A SECOND CHANCE AT LIFE

A SECOND CHANCE AT LIFE

Brian Huynh Travis

Library of Congress Control Number:		2010904914
ISBN:	Hardcover	978-1-4500-7636-4
	Softcover	978-1-4500-7635-7
	Ebook	978-1-4500-7637-1

This book was printed in the United States of America.

To order additional copies of this book, contact:
Xlibris Corporation
1-888-795-4274
www.Xlibris.com
Orders@Xlibris.com
75102

Contents

To my mother and father, who gave me life

and

To America, for giving me a second chance

Acknowledgments

My mother, Pham Thi Be, for being the greatest mother on earth;

Joy Wilson Huynh Travis, for being a wonderful and loving wife who has stood strongly by me through my two military deployments;

My daughters, Briana, Brittany, Braelyn, and Brynnleigh, the greatest gifts I have ever received;

Binh Huynh Dinh, for her selfless sacrifices on the boat journey and being a loving sister;

Son Huynh, for being a caring brother and was also always there when I needed him;

Nancy and Tom Nguyen for sponsoring me, Binh, and Son to the greatest country on Earth and also for taking care of us in the early years;

Robert Salter for editing my articles in Iraq;

I'd also like to thank my wife Joy and Brother-in-Law Tom Jankovic for taking the time to assist in the editing of this book;

Clark Taylor for inspiring me to write my story;

All the Vietnamese boat people who tragically perished on high seas during their escape attempt.

The Beginning

SOMETIME ON A dark fateful night on May 19, 1970, my mom felt her water break and immediately had my dad call for a taxi to take her to the local hospital so that she could deliver me out to this wonderful place we call Earth. But I was impatient and could not wait to see what this wonderful place was all about, so I somehow wiggled my way out while inside the taxi. After everything was done, I weighed almost ten pounds and was twenty-one-inches-long. My parents named me Hung Van Huynh. I was the youngest of eight children in my family. My father had a son from a prior marriage, so there were actually nine of us. My parents' names were Huynh Van Thanh and Pham Thi Be. I had two brothers, Thai and Son. Thai attempted to escape from Vietnam on a boat in 1977, but we have never heard from him again. We presumed Thai had somehow died during his escape attempt. I had five sisters, starting with the oldest first: Minh, Tan, My, Hoa, and Binh. Hoa passed away sometime in 1995, in Vietnam, due to health issues.

My parents owned and operated a fish sauce factory, located in Phu Hai, which was approximately thirty minutes away from our hometown, Phan Thiet. We were southeast of the capital, Saigon. It would take approximately three hours to get to Saigon by car. The fish sauce factory was built sometime in 1973, and it was located right next to a small river, which made it very convenient for fishing boats to drop off their catch to my parents' factory. The factory was named after my two older brothers, "Nouc Mam Thai-Son." It was approximately twenty thousand square feet and had many large wooden storage and refinishing tanks. On the side of the factory, my parents had a modest home by the river. Nothing beats a summer breeze in Phu Hai and the views of the river were spectacular during the twilight hours, as you hear the waves murmuring at the foot of our house. In the garden, to the rear of the factory, my parents had grown rows after rows of guava. My mother and I would take leisurely strolls in our guava garden and pick out the best guava for us to snack on.

My parents had worked very hard to get this factory up-and-running. They borrowed and pretty much begged from everyone to get enough money together to have it built and purchased just enough equipment to begin operation. Because of their hard work, devotion, passion, and intimate knowledge on fish-sauce-making techniques, the factory began producing one of the best fish sauces in Vietnam. My parents employed approximately six locals to help them with their everyday operation. My parents were really kind and good to these folks. I remembered they used to roast a pig every so often and had a feast to show appreciation for their employees. My parents had big aspirations of bottling the fish sauce and exporting it to nearby countries.

However, at the time, Vietnam was in the midst of a brutal war-pitting communist North, supported by its allies, against the United States-backed democratic South. Of course, I did not know much about this war until I read about it while going through middle school in the history class and then later on in life, when I did some more research into the conflict. From what I have read, the United States entered the war to prevent a communist takeover of South Vietnam as part of their wider strategy of containment. The U.S. military advisors arrived in the South in 1950. The U.S. involvement escalated in the early 1960s, with U.S. troop levels tripling in 1961 and tripling again in 1962 (1). The U.S. combat units were deployed beginning in 1965, and their involvement peaked in 1968 at the time of the "Tet Offensive." After this offensive, the U.S. ground forces were withdrawn as part of a policy called "Vietnamization" (2).

In 1973, the governments of the Democratic Republic of Vietnam (North Vietnam), the Republic of Vietnam (South Vietnam), and the United States, as well as the Provisional Revolutionary Government (PRG) that represented indigenous South Vietnamese revolutionaries signed the agreement on ending the war and restoring peace in Vietnam. The agreement was called the Paris Peace Accords, and it was signed on January 27, 1973, at the Majestic Hotel in Paris (3).

The accords called for an in-place ceasefire. North and South Vietnamese forces were to hold their locations. Both sides were permitted to resupply military materials to the extent necessary to replace items consumed in the course of the truce. As soon as the ceasefire came into effect, U.S. troops, along with other foreign soldiers, would begin to withdraw, with the withdrawal to be completed within sixty days. Simultaneously, U.S. prisoners of war would be released and allowed to return home. The parties to the agreement agreed to assist in repatriating the remains of the dead.

There would be negotiations between the two South Vietnamese parties, who were Saigon and the Vietcong, toward a political settlement that would allow the South Vietnamese people to decide themselves the political future of South Vietnam through genuinely free and democratic general elections under international supervision. And the last provision in the accords stated reunification of Vietnam was to be "carried out step-by-step through peaceful means."

However, as suspected there were numerous violations to the Paris Peace Accords committed by both sides. President Nixon and the United States had promised South Vietnamese President Nguyen Van Thieu that it would use airpower to support his government and resume bombing in North Vietnam if the North launched a major offensive against South Vietnam. However, President Nixon was driven from office due to the Watergate scandal in 1974, and when the North Vietnamese did begin the final offensive in early 1975, the United States Congress refused to appropriate the funds needed by the South Vietnamese, and because of this the South completely collapsed.

The North Vietnamese entered Saigon on April 30, 1975. At 8:35 a.m. that morning, the final ten Marines from the U.S. Embassy departed by chopper (4).

It seemed like my memory bank did not start working until I was almost five years old. The first memory I can recall was sometime in early April 1975. I can still remember standing outside my parents' fish sauce factory in Phu Hai, when I heard gunshots ring out nearby. My mom ran up, swooped me off my feet, and brought me inside our house to hide.

About an hour later, after my parents determined the danger was over, we exited our house to see what had happened. The situation was still very chaotic. The town's people were running and screaming about in the streets. And as we approached our front gate, we saw two South Vietnamese army soldiers lying dead near the road leading to our driveway. I later learned from my parents that apparently the North Vietnamese troops had caught up to some retreating South Vietnamese soldiers and a fierce firefight ensued. It was obvious the North Vietnamese soldiers won this firefight, because I saw about six of them telling my parents and nearby villagers that our town had been liberated from the corrupt government forces of the South. It was my first time ever laying eyes on soldiers from the north. The soldiers continued on with more instructions on what my parents and others needed to do in the coming days in order to be in compliance with their directives. They told my parents and others that their comrades were on their way to liberating Saigon and the rest of the country.

They said they would take the country back from the rich and give it to the poor. The North soldiers continued to tell my parents and the other people not to do anything "stupid" and to cooperate with them fully, and everything would be fine in a few days.

After receiving instructions from the soldiers, my parents returned to their factory. Standing outside our main house attached to the factory, my father said to my mother that he had a bad feeling about the statement one of the soldiers made about taking from the rich to give to the poor. Though my parents were not rich by western standards, they were definitely considered very rich by the communist North. Viet Nam was and still is a third world country and by Vietnamese standards, if you own a car, store, factory, or any other luxury items, you were considered "rich."

Shortly after, Saigon and the rest of South Viet Nam fell to the communist North. It wasn't long after that they started to intern most South Vietnamese soldiers into these so-called re-education camps.

The Communists Took Everything from My Parents

A FEW MONTHS later, the city officials from Phu Hai and two police officers arrived at my parents' factory and announced that they had a week to move all their belongings out, and the factory would be confiscated from them for the benefit of the community. They ordered my parents that they had to report to a re-education camp the day after they moved out. They told my parents that after the completion of their re-education camp, we would be relocated to a "New Economic Zone," an area far away from our home to start over. They said we had to live off the land, a punishment at the time for what they deemed "rich people." By no means were my parents rich. They had a little bit of money, but that was because they had worked hard all their lives to save up whatever they had. However, in the communist North, they viewed the little amount of money my parents had as a lot. After we were forced to move out, we learned from our old neighbors that the mayor of Phu Hai moved him and his family into our nice home next to the fish sauce factory. This contradicted the communists' propaganda that they would take from the rich and share it with the poor. That was not the case at all. They lied. But then again what else is new?

Freedom at All Risks—the Journey Begins

RIGHT BEFORE AND immediately after the fall of Saigon, people were leaving or trying to leave Vietnam by the boatloads, literally. They were known as the "boat people." Because the communists deemed my family was "rich," they had blacklisted all of us from being accepted into any good schools in the area or obtaining any good paying jobs. At the time, all of my brothers and sisters had no jobs and the prospect of getting a job anywhere in Vietnam, being on this blacklist, was very slim to every one of us. My parents realized this and had to make the toughest decisions of their lives and that was to get all of us on these boats that were leaving Vietnam so that we could have a chance of freedom and a prosperous life. But these boats that were leaving at the time were not free. Every seat on these boats sometimes came with a very high monetary price. It could cost anywhere from hundreds to thousands of U.S. dollars, depending on who you knew.

But the highest price of all would be one's life. Of course, my parents knew of the inherent dangers that awaited us once we were on high seas. They have heard of many stories of desperate boat people getting robbed, raped, beaten up, and even murdered by the sea pirates on top of having to deal with the natural hardships of starvation, thirst, and hunger. However, my parents knew that they had to take the ultimate risk so that we could have a second chance at life.

Sometime in 1977, my parents were desperate to get my brother Thai out Vietnam. He would be the first from our family to embark on the dangerous journey. At the time, he was in his early twenties and eager to work and earn money. However, his future was bleak, because in Vietnam and under communism, you had to know someone in high places to get a good job. Besides, he was about to be drafted into the North Vietnamese Army and my parents did not want that, and neither did my brother Thai.

With this in mind, my parents decided Thai had to leave and leave now. They managed to borrow enough money to buy him a seat on the next boat leaving Vietnam. Everything was kept really secretive, because no one wanted to be arrested before their chance of escaping or get their family members arrested for conspiring to plan an escape. The punishments for these crimes were very severe. If word got out that you were trying to escape, the local police would come knocking on your door one night and that would be the last time you hear of that person again. So when my brother Thai left, I never got to say good-bye to him. I didn't even know he left until a week later when I asked my mom where he was.

At first, she did not want to tell me the truth, fearing I might tell my friends and the police would find out. That could cause a lot of problems for our already troubled family. But after a few moments of silence, she decided to tell me that Thai had to go somewhere far away to get a job and that he would write us soon.

I believed her and went back to playing with my friends. However, days, weeks, and months went by without a word from him. But I was too young to pay attention to something like this. My worry at the time was just playing soccer with my friends and having a good time. However, one night I returned home from a friend's house and saw my mother sitting at our little kitchen table crying uncontrollably. My father was in the back of our house appearing to stare at the stars. I quickly ran up to my mother to see why she was crying. I was definitely a mama's boy. She quickly hugged me and asked me if I had fun playing at my friend's house. I knew she was trying to avoid my question, but I was very persistent. I kept asking her why she was crying and if there was anything I could do to make her stop.

I loved my mother with all my heart and to see her crying just really hurt me. I wanted to know because I thought someone had hurt her, and I wanted to beat them up if that was the case. A typical young boy's thinking I guess. She kept looking at me with her soft, motherly stare and gentle smile. It took a little while for her to tell me the truth. She told me she has not heard from Thai since the day he left and that something terribly wrong might have happened to him. She just missed him dearly and wished he was still here with us.

I told her I was sorry that she was in so much pain and wished that there was something I could do to make her stop crying. She said softly that she appreciated my concern and that she loved me very much. Then she told me it was getting late and I needed to get ready for bed. I went to sleep that night with a lot on my mind. At first, I tossed and turned while thinking about my brother. I kept asking myself what could have happened to my brother. I remembered thinking why he had to go so far to get a job. I was really puzzled, but tiredness set in a short time later, and I fell asleep.

The next day I approached my mother again about Thai. I could tell that she barely got any sleep the night before because her eyes were bloodshot and she just appeared exhausted. I asked her, "Ma, please tell me what happened to Thai. Is he okay?" She sat me down at our kitchen table and finally told me the truth. She told me Thai tried to escape from Vietnam on a boat about ten months ago, but she has not heard anything from him. She was crying because she had a bad dream about him the other night. She said that in her dream Thai died on high seas. She said she even heard him call out for her in her dream. She told me when a person had that type of dream, it was never good.

As I was sitting there talking with my mother, my father came back into our house from the back, and he too appeared to have been up all night grieving over the possible death of Thai. He did not say anything to me. He has always been the type that held things inside. He did smile at me and asked how I was doing. I told him I was not doing so well because they were not doing well. He gently patted me on the top of my head as he walked by on his way out the front door. I did not know where he was going because he did not have a job at the time. We stayed at this small town for another year or so until we moved back to Phu Hai and lived with my oldest sister, Minh, and her children. There, I would spend the days playing in the salt fields with my new friends, since we did not have to go to school.

I remembered one day my friends and I went up on this hill overlooking the sea. It was really beautiful from where we were at. We just sat there and talked about how we wished we could leave Vietnam and go to America. We have always heard from our elders that America was the land of opportunities and you were free to speak your mind whenever you wanted. That is so contrary to Vietnam. If you were caught speaking badly about communism and how corrupt they were, your punishment could range from a beating to facing a firing squad for sedition.

Living with Minh and her children was great. However, my parents could not give her enough money to feed us all every day. So, food was always a hot commodity for our family. There were some days where we had rice and fresh fish for dinner. Other days, we barely had enough rice and very little vegetables for everyone.

Now, it was around February 1979 or so. Unbeknownst to me, my parents had scraped up just enough money to buy three seats on a small boat that was scheduled to make an attempt to escape from Vietnam. I went on doing my own thing every day, as if everything was just fine and dandy.

BRIAN HUYNH TRAVIS

Then one night, my brother, Son, and my sister, Binh, the youngest of my five sisters, told me I had to go with them *somewhere*. I was not sure where that *somewhere* would be at the time. We met up with some strangers at a small boat dock in Phu Hai. I don't remember where it was exactly. However, I do remember getting into this very small taxi boat and was told to lie down in the underneath compartment and not to move a muscle. So, we all got on the boat and complied with the boat rower's orders. I still did not really know what was going on at the time, but I realized whatever we were about to embark on was not normal.

The stranger told us he would have to make one stop before taking us to the main boat. Apparently, that one stop was to ferry some soldiers across the river. I didn't think anything of that until the soldiers boarded our taxi boat. Then my heart started beating faster and harder. Though I was still young at the time, I still knew what would happen to us if the soldiers discovered we were hiding in the underneath compartment, and our ultimate goal was to try to escape from Vietnam. It would have certainly been a long jail sentence for all of us, or even death.

But luckily, everything worked out just fine, and we finally made it to the main boat. By now, I knew that I was about to embark on a long and dangerous journey escaping from Vietnam. However, it did not hit me yet as I climbed onto this small wooden boat. I remembered thinking there were too many people on this boat because I was rubbing shoulders with strangers and barely had enough room to move my arms. Somehow, we all managed to get on, and the boat pulled away from the wharf and began to set out to sea.

Our boat quietly departed the small river in the ghostly darkness of a late February night in 1979, hoping to find our way to Malaysia or Singapore. There were thirty of us on board a thirty-foot wooden boat, that was not seaworthy, with very little water and food. We were of all ages, sizes, some dispirited, but most were happy, and brimming with hope that we would reach our destination. The sky was clear and the stars shone brightly. The boat rocked slightly on the waves and continued to run at its full speed. I looked back at the shore and saw whatever little lights I could see fade into the night. Then there were no more lights, just the eerie darkness of the sea. Everyone on the boat knew so well at the time that there was no going back. Either we would make it to Malaysia or Singapore or die somewhere in the immense and unforgiving sea.

That was when it dawned on me that I might not ever get to see my parents again. I felt this terrible sadness within. I felt so helpless and lonely. It was so bad that it became hard for me to breathe. I began to cry uncontrollably, screaming out for my mother. My sister, Binh, grabbed me and held on to me tightly while telling me that our parents wanted us to have a future and that was the reason why they sent us on this perilous journey. She reassured me that our parents would meet up with us very soon.

Even though she knew the odds of our parents successfully escaping from Vietnam in the near future to meet up with us were very slim, she still had to say it to get me to quiet down. Though we were now far from land, North Vietnamese patrol boats could be nearby, and if they hear my cry, they would certainly arrest us or even worse, execute us right there and then. They have been known to do that in the past since they did have orders to shoot and kill any escapees on the spot. Then I started to feel nauseous, and the next thing I knew I was leaning over the boat feeding the fish. Actually, I spent the next few hours feeding the fish with whatever I had for dinner.

Soon, I could not feed the fish or cry any longer due to being exhausted from everything that had happened so far. So I fell asleep. Morning came and it was a beautiful day. The sea was calm and I no longer felt nauseous or seasick. I remembered sitting next to my sister and brother in the small boat cabin gazing out at the sea. The ocean was lovely. It was a deep-blue color. As our boat moved forward, from time to time a small fish would fly out of its way. There were a few occasions where dolphins would swim almost side by side with our boat. It was the first time I could actually see everyone on board. I saw my sister writing something in a small notepad, so I asked what she was doing. She told me she was keeping a journal of our journey. I gave her a smile of approval.

I looked around and could see there were approximately twenty-five males and five females, my sister included, aboard this small and cramped boat. I tried to stretch my legs as they were cramped from being drawn up all night into such a small space. My clothes felt damp and clammy, but that was the only clothing I had. We did not bring any change of clothing, since we were not allowed to because of the small boat we were traveling in. Then one of the men called for everyone's attention. I took it that he was the captain of the boat. He began telling us we did not have a lot of food and water on board the boat and that we had to ration our food right away. He told us there would be no washing of any kind with the drinking water, because the water will be more and more precious to us than anything else as we continue on with our journey.

He stated if everything went as planned, we would arrive in Malaysia in less than one week. That didn't sound too bad. At worst, we would spend just seven days on high sea, I thought. He continued to tell us that everyone on the boat will get two cups of water a day and one small bowl of cooked rice for lunch and dinner.

Needless to say that morning we did not get cooked rice to eat. However, I was not hungry anyway. My fear of the uncertainty and the unknown lingered in my mind. I kept asking myself, "Are we heading in the right direction? Will we make it to Malaysia?" Will we survive from being out here with very little food and water? Where will we end up if we get lost at sea?

I remember getting two small bowls of rice that night. I asked my sister how come I got two bowls while everyone else got just one. She reminded me that I told her I was not hungry at lunch time, so she saved that bowl of rice for me so that I could eat both at dinner time. For some reason I was still not hungry, but she encouraged me to eat it so that I could have the strength to go on. I agreed and ate the rice with a little bit of canned sardine that came with the evening rice bowl. What a treat that was. I should have been content, but I was still very melancholy. I kept thinking about my parents and how badly I was missing them. As the realization of a long separation from them sank in, perhaps months, possibly years, I quickly veered toward panic and then settled into depression. I was in and out of depression for the next day or two.

On our third day, dark clouds hovered overhead, and strong winds started to blow heavily against our tiny wooden boat. The boat pitched and tossed as though it was climbing a hill only to fall down on the other side. The calm ocean became increasingly violent with ferocious waves driving our boat far off course. There was no land in sight, nothing except the rumbling sky, the quivering winds, and our fast-trembling heartbeats. Some people began crying while others prayed for the sea to calm down. When you are on a small wooden boat on the high seas in the middle of nowhere, the last thing you want to see is violent waves. I asked myself if we were going to make it through the storm or would we be taken by the sea. I asked my sister if we would be okay. She calmly told me something to the effect of, "Yes. Don't worry my brother. We have God and the Holy Spirits on our sides. They will protect us from danger. You will see." It was like an angel had come and told her that God was protecting us from the storm and that nothing would seriously hurt us from this journey. Soon, the sea began to calm down and the winds withered away. The waves became gentle again, and the clouds dissipated. The next few days were very uneventful as we wandered about on the high seas like young children visiting the zoo for the first time.

The seventh day came without any excitement. There was still no land in sight or any talk of arriving in Malaysia from any of the men. I looked up and saw the same man, the captain, huddled with some other older people on our boat near the bow. They were talking about something, but by the look on their faces, I knew it couldn't be anything good. Soon after they adjourned their meeting, the captain got everyone's attention and made another announcement. He told us the storm from three days ago knocked us off course, and now he was not sure where we were. To make things worse, we did not have any compasses on board, so they were guiding this boat by unknown means.

The captain reassured us he would get us back on course, but that was not his main concern. He said his main concern was we were running out of rice, water, and fuel, although we had enough to last us for a few more days. The fish that they had been catching, our main source of nourishment, was also drying up. I did not know how to digest the information I just heard. I asked my sister what all that meant, and again she reassured me that the captain would get us to Malaysia soon and for me not to worry.

After a week on the high seas, the trip has undermined everyone's health. Our clothes were always wet from the spray of the ocean waves, because our boat was so small and the side of the boat was almost at sea level. Our spirits and strength were greatly diminished also.

On the eighth day during the morning hours, I was really thirsty. It had been almost sixteen hours ago when I received a small cup of water along with a small bowl of rice for lunch. My lips were really dry and chapped. My tongue was like a piece of sandpaper against the inner walls of my mouth. I kept asking my sister if she could get me some water, because I was really thirsty. She tried to get me some water but was denied by the captain of the boat. He kept telling her that we were really low on water and for me to hang in there until we could reach land. I thought to myself that I would probably not make it by the next day if I didn't get any water soon. As I lay there haplessly waiting for a miracle, my sister and brother began to cry loudly knowing that if I didn't get any water soon I might not make it through the night.

Finally, it was sometime in the early afternoon that we got our small bowl of rice and a very small amount of water along with it. My sister gave me her portion of the water. I was so happy while downing a little more than three gulps of water. I had never been so happy to drink just a little bit of water before. But reality set in after my five seconds of happiness that our survival was looking bleaker and bleaker by the minute.

As the darkness fell upon us that night, people on our tiny boat were starting to get very desperate. There would be no food or water that night for us. I had a feeling that if we didn't find landfall soon, then death would be awaiting us within the next few days. I prayed and prayed to God and the Holy Spirits to come and rescue us from this dire situation. My prayers were answered when a Thai fishing ship spotted us and made their approach. I remembered seeing many bright lights coming from a distance. As the lights got closer, I could see this huge fishing ship. It must have been at least a hundred feet long. The ship pulled up to our small boat, and a few Thai fishermen boarded our ship.

I was not sure what was said between our boat captain and the Thai fishermen, but I am sure it went something like this, "We don't have any food or water and we beg you to give us some. Please. Please." In the end, I saw our captain hand the Thai fishermen some jewelry, and in return they gave us a bag or two of rice, a couple jugs of water, and some fuel for our boat. Our captain thanked them endlessly before our ships went separate ways. We were all so happy that night. For the next few days, we were given some water and rice for lunch and dinner. There were a few days when some guys would jump into the sea and actually catch fish for our boat. They shared the fish they caught and we ate them raw, like sushi.

We were still lost on high seas and landfall was no where in sight. On our twentieth or twenty-first day, we started to run out of rice and water again. By now, most of us were too weak to make a big stink about it. We were all in a daze, and that feeling of hopelessness was abundant. Most of us began to beg for food and water again. I remembered going almost two days without any food and only with a little bit of water each day. I began to think about death and that I would not be able to say good-bye to my parents. I thought this was not the way I wanted to die. I was only eight at the time and wished for a second chance at life. I began to pray to God and the Holy Spirits again to come and rescue us.

My prayers were answered once more. It appeared another Thai fishing ship had spotted us and was making its way toward us. It was in the afternoon at the time. As the ship got closer, I could see that this fishing ship was not as big as the first one. They pulled up alongside of us, and they did not appear to be as friendly as the first Thai fishing ship either. This time approximately ten Thai fishermen jumped onto our small boat. It appeared that they had spears and other weapons in their hands. One of them demanded to speak to the captain, while the others were checking us out. After a few minutes, I saw they were collecting jewelry and other items from people on our boat. That was when I realized these were the Thai pirates that the people on our boat had been talking about. I vaguely remembered from overhearing their conservations that Thai pirates were ruthless and that they usually rob the boat people of their belongings, rape the women, and then kill everyone by sinking their boats.

Again, thoughts of death went through my mind. I definitely did not want to be food for the sharks and that was not another way I had envisioned I would die. With whatever strength I had been left with, I sat up and watched them very closely as they were grabbing things from our people. They then all returned to their boat. I thought now we were all going to die broke after being robbed. I had a vision that they were going to ram our boat with their ship. At least they left my sister and the other four women on our boat alone. Then something happened that I never thought would come from pirates. They threw us a bag of rice, a couple five-gallon water cans, and a little bit of fuel.

We were very happy to receive the rice, water, and fuel. I believed the people on our boat would have gladly exchanged their jewelry and other valuables for rice and water without being robbed first. Anyway, we were just happy to get anything from them at all. That night we had food for the first time in almost two days. We were just anxious and praying to see land soon. All of us knew we would not last another week out here like this.

A few days later, on a pitch-black night, we finally saw something we had been looking for, and that was land. We saw on the horizon shadows of lights, a lot of lights. As we got closer, it seemed it was from another world. We were all very excited. Many of us cried. There was a sense of relief that you could never describe. We didn't care if the lights were from a town in Malaysia, Singapore, Philippines, or Mars. We just wanted to get off this rickety boat and eat some real food and drink as much water as we wanted.

Then we spotted another ship. This one had a lot of lights too, and it appeared to be very big—a lot bigger than the other two Thai fishing ships that we had encountered. And it was coming at us pretty fast. As it got closer, I heard our captain say it was a military ship. We weren't sure which navy it belonged to. It pulled up and we realized it was the Malaysian Coast Guard ship. A small contingent of their sailors boarded our small boat. With the sailors was a Vietnamese interpreter. The interpreter told our captain that their country no longer had anymore room for boat refugees from Vietnam. They apologized for having to deny us entry, and also according to their orders, they would have to tow us back out to high seas.

We were all devastated as the captain relayed the message to us. The sailors did say they were authorized to provide us with some food and water and pointed us to the direction of Indonesia where that country was still accepting

BRIAN HUYNH TRAVIS

boat refugees. We begged the sailors to allow us to dock, but they adamantly refused and said that they had orders.

The captain said there was nothing we could do but comply with their orders. The sailors then threw us a line and told the captain to tie it to our boat's stern. Keep in mind this coast guard ship is very big compared to our thirty-foot boat. They began to tow our boat back out to sea. But as their ship was accelerating, our ship's stern appeared like it was sinking really fast into the sea. I guess this is due to the pressure of being pulled very fast by a much larger ship. We all panicked and screamed for the coast guard ship to slow down. However, they did not hear us and continued at their current speed.

Thank God to our fast-thinking captain who grabbed a very big knife and began cutting the line. If it wasn't for his fast thinking, our boat would have sunk, and I am pretty certain I wouldn't be here sharing my story. After the line was cut, the coast guard ship turned around and pulled up next to our boat to ask why we cut the line. Our captain explained to them what had happened, and they requested we would follow them out to international waters. Our captain agreed. Soon we were again on the high seas in the pitch-black night with only a verbal direction, from a Vietnamese interpreter, on which direction to head should we want to try and land in Indonesia. So on we went in that direction. But for some reason, it took us about four days to get there.

On the morning of our thirtieth day, we again saw landfall. We were very excited like we had just won the lottery. We were pretty certain this was Indonesia. Or at least we were praying that it was not some other country that was not accepting boat refugees. As we got closer and closer to the land, we did not see any coast guard ships anywhere.

We arrived at a maze of small islands. The captain confirmed we had in fact arrived in Indonesia. We went through what seemed like hundreds of these small islands. However, we had not seen any sign of life on these islands. Then in front of us, there was an island that was bigger than most, and it appeared there were people there. We later learned this refugee camp was called "Batam Pulau Galang."

As our boat approached this island to dock, we were given a warm, yet strange welcome by other refugees. Some came up to our boat and asked us if we needed help. Some looked but walked away. Some appeared to be too tired to even care. We disembarked our boat and touched land for the first time in thirty days. God, that was a great feeling. I felt so lucky to have survived that journey that I prayed for days. I thanked God and the Holy Spirits countless times for protecting us and keeping us safe on that boat. To have survived in a small wooden boat for thirty days with thirty people and with very little food, water, and fuel was just a miracle.

But our journey continued on. There were no breaks at this point. Now we had to find a place to live in, food to eat, and someone to speak to so that we could apply for political asylum to the United States. Luckily, there were people from the Red Cross who helped us by placing us in a small shack. They also provided us with food and water, and some clothing. I was so happy to get out of my pair of pants and t-shirt I had been wearing for the past thirty days. I went and washed up with the soap that was given to me. You wouldn't want to be next to any of us at this time. We definitely did not smell like a rose garden.

After we cleaned up and ate real food for the first time in thirty days, the Red Cross personnel directed us to the office of the United Nations High Commission for Refugees (UNHCR), which was also located on the same island. There, we wrote to Aunt Nancy Nguyen and Uncle Tom Nguyen, who were living in California at the time. Uncle Tom was a Major in the South Vietnamese Air Force and in the waning days of April 1975—he and his family were evacuated to an American ship, waiting right outside of Saigon. They were later flown to California, where they were given political-asylum status.

While we were waiting for our UNHCR to process our asylum application, we wrote to our parents back home to let them know that we had arrived in Indonesia safely. My parents must have been worried to death, just waiting to hear from us. The letters we wrote did reach my parents and they wrote us back shortly after. The mail process took just over two weeks, and we finally got their letter. Just as I expected, they felt very blessed that we survived the boat trip and were now in Indonesia awaiting acceptance from the United States. Despite having my sister and brother take care of me, I missed my parents terribly.

Just imagine an eight-year-old child with a seventeen-year-old brother and a twenty-one-year-old sister wondering about the safety of our family members back in Vietnam. I wandered about the island day in, day out. Since the island was newly established because of the influx of the boat people, there were no schools set up yet to try to prepare us for our new homeland. I made new friends and remembered them telling me of how some of the people on their boat had died, while others were raped by Thai pirates. I felt so blessed that nothing really bad happened to us, even though our boat was boarded twice by Thai pirates and was only robbed of materialistic things once, compared to what had happened to some of the other boats.

Our application for the asylum process took approximately six months. But it seemed like it lasted forever. Everyday seemed so long and it just appeared to drag on and on. I remembered sitting by one of the makeshift boat docks looking out into the ocean and just wishing we would get accepted by the United States. Then one day sometime in late October 1979, we were informed by UNHCR officials that we have been granted political asylum in the United States. That was another one of the happiest days of our lives. The United States was definitely the country we had wished to go to for a second chance at life. Are you kidding me, the United States was and still is the greatest country on earth to live in. It was also convenient that our aunt and uncle were also living there. Having family around would make the transition a little better.

The process of getting us to the United States was actually pretty quick. A few days after receiving the great news of being accepted to go to the United States, we and a few other families that were also granted political asylum were transported to Jakarta, the capital of Indonesia, for a scheduled flight. I remembered the feelings of relief, happiness, excitement, and euphoria as I boarded the boat that was taking us to another island so that we could be driven to the capital for our flight. As our boat pulled away from the island, I looked back and saw there were so many other refugees left behind. Some would be leaving soon, while others would have to wait longer. One thing was for certain and that was more boat people would be arriving soon. And more would die trying to find that second chance at life.

We arrived in Jakarta a few hours later. This was the first time I had ever seen a real airport. It looked enormous with so many buildings. There, planes were taking off and landing every minute. I was just amazed at everything I was seeing that day. I don't think it had actually hit me yet that I was finally going to board a plane and fly to the United States. We waited for a few more hours before the moment of truth came. Our group was provided some last-minute instructions by UNHCR members before one of them led us down this tunnel. I held my sister's hand firmly as we arrived at the plane. There was a feeling of relief and happiness that set in. I kept asking myself if this could be real. Could I really be going to the United States?

Final Destination, Travis Air Force Base, California

IT WAS IN early November 1979 that our plane touched down at Travis Air Force Base in Fairfield. I can repeat with unabashed and proud candor that I kissed the tarmac of Travis Air Force Base after we debarked our plane. It was a chilly morning. I don't recall experiencing any temperature below seventy degrees Fahrenheit while living in Vietnam. But I didn't care. I was just happy to be here. We were congratulated by UNHCR members and the crew of the plane. Our group was then ushered to the terminal, where my uncle and aunt were happily waiting. My uncle and aunt had sent us pictures of themselves while we were living on the island, so we could recognize them after we got off the plane. As soon as we saw them, we waved to them, and they ran toward us. We saw that and so we ran toward them. It was a beautiful moment. We all embraced each other dearly for a while. My sister and brother cried in joy. I was just so happy. I didn't know if I should cry or scream at the time, so I just hugged them while sporting the biggest smile I could have on my face.

UNHCR members provided my aunt and uncle additional paperwork for us and instructed them on where they needed to take us in order to complete the immigration process. We thanked them endlessly before parting ways.

My aunt and uncle introduced us to their three children, Peter, Linda, and David. They were the same ages as we were. They then drove us back to their house in San Mateo. They were living in a modest home on Humboldt Street at the time. They said that my brother and I would be staying in Peter's and David's room, while my sister was to stay with Linda. The living arrangement was temporary until the government could find us housing in the area. She then drove us around and showed us the downtown San Mateo area. It was evening time, so the downtown area was lit up beautifully. There were many people walking about. The streets were very clean and abounded with cars. It was just an amazing first impression of this great country. She told us Tom and she were hairstylists and owned a barbershop on the 100 block of B Street in downtown San Mateo. It was called "Saigon Barbershop." She took us there and showed us around her shop. We stayed there for about half an hour before she took us to a local supermarket to buy groceries. As soon as I walked in the store, I was just amazed and shocked to see every shelf stocked to the brim with merchandise and the produce section replete with so many different fruits and vegetables. I was salivating just by looking at the variety of food in the store. Everyone was so nice and polite and so orderly. This was a big contrast to how people shop in Vietnam.

I remembered a few times when my mom took me to the market in Phantiet and it seemed everyone was so unruly. They all cut in front of each other while trying to pay. There was absolutely no line at all at these markets or shops in Vietnam. This was obviously very strange to me to see everyone so orderly, so I asked my aunt about it. She explained to me that in America, people stand in line when they buy things or try to get services. People stop and help you with directions when you are lost. Most people obey the laws of the land. When driving in this country, drivers obey traffic laws and posted traffic signs. Pedestrians normally cross the street in crosswalks, pay their taxes, and pick up after themselves. She said she would teach us these new customs in the next few days so that we would not offend anyone or get into trouble by not knowing what to do. After buying our groceries, we returned home and made dinner that night. After dinner, my uncle turned on the television and introduced me to the game of football. We watched the Atlanta Falcons play against the Los Angeles Rams. At first, I thought it was a weird and violent game with men wearing pads and helmets and tackling each other all over the place. But my uncle thoroughly explained to me how the game was played, so by the fourth quarter, I was starting to get a grasp of this new game called "football." After the game, we all stayed up talking for hours before going to sleep. That night, I did not sleep very well, because I was badly missing my parents. I knew that the passage to adulthood involved growing up here. I had a gut feeling that it would not be easy starting from scratch, especially with the additional burdens associated with the sudden flight from my former homeland. I wished my parents were here with me as I began the greatest challenge in my new life here in this great country.

The Assimilation Process and Growing Up in America Begins

F IRST THING WAS first; my aunt thought it was very important for us to address the issue of respect when speaking to our elders here in America. In the Vietnamese culture and custom, we would always address our elders and others appropriately. For example, in Vietnam, I had to address my older brothers by saying "Anh" before saying their first names or my older sisters by saying "Chi" in front of their first names to show respect. In my case, I had been calling my brother "Anh Son" and my sister "Chi Binh" before I would begin speaking to them. If I didn't do that, it would be deemed disrespectful and I would be scorned for it. When I spoke to my aunt and uncle or my other relatives back in Vietnam, I had to use the appropriate title at all times. Also, if you were addressing a friend, or even a stranger who was older than you, then you would have to address them appropriately according to their perceived age. For example, if I was addressing a family friend who was the same age as my uncle, I would call him "Chu" before his name. "Chu" means the same as uncle, but "Chu" usually was used for someone who was not your blood uncle.

My aunt brought up the point that in America, we don't really address our older brothers or older sisters by saying "Brother" or "Sister" before we say their names. It would cause some confusion in the people we are speaking to. She said for example if we use "Brother" in front of someone's name when addressing them, they could take the "Brother" to refer to a priest or monk. Or if you use, "Sister" before a person's name when addressing that person, it would mean she was a nun or it could offend African Americans, if they perceived you as making fun of them. So my aunt, brother, and sister spent approximately half an hour on this subject, and when it was all over, they decided I would have to say "Aunt Nancy," "Uncle Tom," "Brother Son," and "Sister Binh," when addressing them. However, I didn't have to address family friends or strangers the same way. Of course, I had no say in that discussion, but I was alright with that, and I didn't think it was a big deal that I had to do that here also. I was not saying anything new that I hadn't said before when addressing my elders, so I began addressing them accordingly in English.

We lived with my aunt and uncle for approximately one month. Though it was great living with them and getting to know them all over again, we wanted to live by ourselves. We wanted to experience having our own place and be independent. We were now receiving welfare and money for low-income-group housing. We received the money on the first of every month. It wasn't much, but it was definitely better than nothing. We found a one bedroom apartment at 139 North Grant Street in San Mateo. We moved in soon after. My sister had her own room while my brother and I slept on the couch, in the living room. We had the bare essentials to survive. In my sister's room she had a mattress and a small used dresser. We did not have any stereo equipment. No VHS or Beta VCR player. We had a small 13" black and white television in the living room that barely worked. We had one phone in the apartment and that was in the kitchen. My brother and I kept whatever clothing we had in cardboard boxes in the living room. But with the little things that we had, it was still better than living in Vietnam, so there were no complaints from us.

We were all just soaking it in, this great land of America. It was also great living on our own. We could come and go as we pleased without having to bother or inconvenience my aunt and uncle. My aunt gave my sister a little bit of money to buy a used car. We were very grateful for their generous gesture. We were really stoked. It was a beat-up car, but it worked, so who cares what it looked like. Prior to having the car, we would use the bus to travel about town or go to the store. My sister would cook for us and do our laundry. My brother and I helped out around the house and took care of all the cleaning duties.

My sister did the best she could to take care of my brother and me. I wouldn't call the area a "Ghetto," but it was definitely a low-income neighborhood. At night we could hear people arguing or fighting nearby and police sirens whaling all night long. My aunt had warned me that we were the only Asian family living in the area that was predominantly African American. She told me to be careful, because she was not certain how they would feel about us living among them. I didn't care. I was just happy to be here, and the great thing about the location was it was a block away from the Martin Luther King Jr. Center, which was located at 725 Monte Diablo Avenue. This was key for me, since I would have to take the yellow bus every morning for school, and it was also the drop-off point for after school. None of us spoke a word of English at the time. My aunt told me I would be attending Beresford Elementary School on the west side of San Mateo. She said I would be in fourth grade because of my age. My aunt told me the school was in a very affluent neighborhood, and there would be a lot of rich kids there. I did not know and did not care where I was supposed to go to school.

I was just happy and excited at the chance to go and learn some English to help me assimilate faster. My aunt also told my brother he was to attend Burlingame High School in Burlingame. And since my sister was already an adult, she was to attend the Adult Day School, located near Aragon High School on Alameda Boulevard, in San Mateo. So we all got our marching orders. My aunt took us to a store, similar to a Wal-Mart, and bought us all school supplies. It was so exciting receiving a backpack, notebooks, pencils, pens, and other cool things for school. She then drove us to a clothing store and bought us some new clothes for school. I couldn't wait for Monday to arrive.

I remembered staying up that Sunday night thinking about school the next morning. Then it dawned on me that the experience could be really bad, since I did not speak any English and had no friends. I was a complete stranger, an immigrant from Vietnam, attending school with these American kids. I looked differently and probably would be dressed differently from the other kids. I was thinking to myself whether I would be accepted or would the kids reject me and make me feel unwanted. There were so many uncertainties that went through my mind. Now, I was not sure anymore if I really wanted to go to school in the morning. So I had a talk with my sister about it. Again my sister knew all the right things to say to reassure me that by going to school it would help us get our parents over here faster. She told us about the sponsorship program where if I become an American citizen I could sponsor family members to come live with me. That was definitely my immediate goal. I missed my parents dearly and if going to school would help me become an American citizen faster, then nothing was going to stand in my way. So I went to sleep that night with that goal in mind.

The next morning, my sister got us up at about six o'clock and told us to get ready for school. My sister told me that my aunt was going to come by seven o'clock to pick me up so that she could take me to Beresford to register me for school. My aunt arrived at our apartment promptly at seven. I got in her car and off we went. As we approached the school, I could see exactly what my aunt meant when she said the school was located in a very affluent area. As I looked around, I saw these houses were so much bigger compared to the ones near the King Center. The streets were much cleaner and the landscaping was well kept. And there were no apartment complexes anywhere nearby. We arrived and my aunt took me into the office. She greeted the receptionist and had a long conversation with her. I was just amazed at how well my aunt spoke English. I wanted so badly to speak English just as well as she could, and I wanted to do it now. I didn't want to have to go through the pain of learning English. I wanted to be able to communicate to my new friends that day.

I had so much to tell my new friends, and I couldn't wait to learn their life stories also. After my aunt completed the registration process, she told me my new life would begin as soon as I go to my first class.

My aunt then gave me a hug and wished me luck. She said I was in good hands with the school staff. She also provided me with a lunch card and said my lunch meals were free. All I would have to do was show the card to the lunch staff, and they would provide me with a meal. Before she left, she also told me that after school a yellow bus would arrive in front of the school to pick me and others from my neighborhood up and take us back home. All of this was overwhelming, but I took it all in. I went to my first class. It was an English as a Second Language (ESL) class. I noticed most of my friends in the class were people from other ethnic groups and that made me feel a little more comfortable. They all came up to me and said hello. Some tried to speak to me, but I could not understand what they were saying, so I just smiled and nodded my head, "Yes. Yes."

Then we had our first break. I went out to the play yard to see what was going on. Not even a minute had passed, when another student came up to me and said hello. He was African American and appeared pretty big for his age. He said his name was Craig. I had never seen or met an African American person before. Craig started talking to me, but I did not understand what he was saying at all. After a while, Craig realized I did not speak a lick of English, so he tried to communicate with me through using his hands. It appeared to me Craig was trying to tell me to walk up to a teacher who was standing nearby and tell the teacher hello. But instead of telling me to say "hello" to the teacher, Craig actually was trying to play a practical joke on me. I could still vividly remember what he told me to say to the teacher. The word was "F-you." I didn't know at the time what that meant. I thought Craig was a nice guy. He had a friendly smile and appeared very believable. I was new to the country and to the school and thought this would be a good way to score points with the teacher, so I did.

I walked right up to the teacher, had a big smile, and waved my hand in a very friendly way. The teacher looked at me pleasantly and smiled back and was waiting for me to say or tell her something. Perhaps she was anticipating

I was going to say good morning or something of that sort. Then the "F-you" word came out of my mouth, and as soon as I said it, I knew something went terribly wrong. Her pleasant smile turned to a shockingly angry look. She started screaming at me and grabbed me by my right arm. She then pulled me with her toward the office.

I had no idea what had just happened, but as I was forcibly being led away, I looked back and saw Craig and others were laughing loudly at the incident. Boy was I mad. I ended up sitting right outside of the assistant principal's office, and everyone inside appeared to be very unfriendly. This was a big contrast compared to when I got there in the morning when everyone was so nice and friendly to me. I sat there and waited. I did not know what or who I was waiting for. A lady walked up to me, said something, and then walked away. Again, she was not very friendly, based on the look she had on her face. It seemed forever, but eventually I saw my aunt walked into the office. At first, I was wondering why she was here to see me again, but when she walked up to me, she told me what had happened. I became even angrier at Craig.

In short, I explained to my aunt the entire story who then translated everything I said to the assistant principal, and she told my aunt she believed me under the circumstances. She asked us to wait for a few seconds while she made a phone call to someone else. I didn't know who she called at the time, but as I was leaving her office, I saw Craig sitting in the same chair. I was just right outside her office, so I knew exactly why he was there. I gave him a dirty look as I was walking away. I never got into trouble for saying F-you to the teacher, thank God. I returned to my class right after.

I was a feisty little guy back in the day. As soon as I was told it was lunch time, I went looking for Craig. I wanted to let him know that I did not appreciate his practical joke. I found him standing with his friends near the cafeteria. I marched right up to him and started cursing him out in Vietnamese. He looked at me and began laughing out loud. That made me even angrier. I began pushing him and challenged him to a fight. Craig looked at me with that look as if to say, "You are crazy to want to fight me. Look at me I will squash you." As I said before, Craig was a lot bigger than I was. I was just a scrawny little Vietnamese boy who grew up without drinking a drop of milk, while Craig probably drank his milk every day. I thought I was Bruce Lee for a moment. I started dancing around, while making crazy sounds like how Bruce Lee did in his movies.

We were about to go at it, when a teacher walked up and told us to break it up. Then another teacher walked up and grabbed me by my right arm and led me to the office once again. Craig was also escorted to the office with me.

BRIAN HUYNH TRAVIS

There, we sat across each other, and from what I could understand we were not to talk to each other and wait for the assistant principal to call us in. I was sitting there thinking to myself something to the effect of, "Are you kidding me. I am back here again. This is only my first day at school. I am definitely going to get into trouble this time." I kept praying that I wouldn't get into trouble and that they would give me a second chance. We sat there for a while, and then I saw my aunt walk into the office again. She did not seem to be very happy for having to return to the school to deal with me for the second time. As soon as my aunt walked up to me, she started telling me she couldn't come here again, because she had to work, and I needed to be a good kid. I felt really badly and apologized to her for my behavior. A short time later, the assistant principal called us both into her office. She spoke to my aunt for a few minutes. From the sound of her tone, I knew she wasn't exchanging pleasantries with my aunt. The assistant principal kept looking at me from time to time during her conversation with my aunt. I was now really worried.

When they were done talking, my aunt turned to me and conveyed what the assistant principal had told her, and that was that the school did not, and would not, tolerate with any fighting. She said we were lucky that we were not fighting this time, or else Craig and I would have both been suspended, and the next violation would be expulsion. There I was just in my first day at school in this great country, and I just got warned that I could be suspended or expelled if there was another violation. Well, feisty or not, I was going to have to chill out and use other means to get back at Craig for getting me into trouble in the first place. After I promised one last time that I would behave, they allowed me to go back to class.

After school, I followed my aunt's instruction and went straight to the bus stop in front of the office. As I was walking up to the bus stop, I saw Craig and his friends standing there waiting for the same yellow bus. I was thinking to myself to be calm and not to do anything stupid. I really didn't want to get kicked out of school at all. I wanted to make my aunt, uncle, brother, and sister proud, so I stood silently next to them. I could feel the tension. It was thicker than concrete. I could feel Craig staring at me. At one point, he said something to me, but I did not understand what he was saying, so I just ignored him. After the yellow bus arrived, I got on last. I sat toward the front, since Craig and his friends occupied the back of the bus. I tried to sit next to other students, but none of them would allow me to sit next to them.

I was afraid what Craig and his friends were going to do to me on the bus. I was even more afraid they would jump me when I got off the bus. There must have been five or six of them. Two of them were females, but they were also big just like Craig.

At some point, I felt a pat on my right shoulder. I was thinking to myself here we go, I'd better get up and try to defend myself. However, when I turned to see what was going on, I saw Craig sitting in the seat behind me. He smiled and said something to me, which I could not understand. But at least he appeared to be friendly. It was a welcoming gesture instead of his fists. I was just happy that he came up and tried to be friendly. Of course, I smiled and just nodded my head. What was I going to say to him? Every word that came out of my mouth would have been in Vietnamese, and I felt that would not be productive anyway, so I just smiled. When we arrived across the street from the Martin Luther King Jr. Center, I got off the bus and Craig walked up to me and followed me home. I lived only a block or so from the Martin Luther King Jr. Center. At first, I did not know if Craig was going to follow me and then try to beat me up or something. So I kept looking back to make sure he wasn't going to jump me. But Craig just kept following me until I got to my apartment. Then he waved bye to me and said something else before he walked on. That was when I realized Craig had just walked me home. He just adopted me of sort. I did not know it at the time, but the area around the Martin Luther King Jr. was really bad.

There was a lot of drug dealing on the corners of Monte Diablo Avenue and North Fremont Street. There were also drive-by shootings from time to time. So I guess Craig was just trying to protect me from the dangers of navigating through these dangerous streets. The next morning, I walked to the bus stop, and Craig and his friends were there. They were friendly to me this time. They said hello. They came up and introduced themselves to me. We became friends from that point on. I will never forget the advice Craig gave to me later that year. He said if you acted like you were scared, then people would pick on you, so try to act tough even if you are scared, and they will leave you alone. He said bad people would always pick on the weak, so be strong. I have always lived by his advice since.

My first December here was pretty interesting and lonely. Up to this point, I have always lived in a tropical climate where the temperature did not get below sixty degrees Fahrenheit. The temperature at the time was somewhere in the high twenties to low thirties at night and in the fifties to sixties during the day in San Mateo. In short, I was freezing my butt off. I felt so lucky I was not living in Minnesota or Wisconsin at the time, because their temperature was well below zero during that time. I just couldn't see myself surviving in those states at all.

BRIAN HUYNH TRAVIS

As my first Christmas here fast approached, I was already wishing for new clothes and toys. I also wanted money because in downtown San Mateo, there was a liquor store that had a few arcade games I loved to play. I remembered I would spend hours watching others play Space Invaders, Frogger, Pacman, and Donkey Kong. Sometimes I had some money and played the games myself, but often I was broke and would just watch others play instead.

My aunt and uncle were nice enough to buy us some new clothes for Christmas, and my sister and brother did end up buying me one or two toys. We did not have money to buy a Christmas tree nor any Christmas decorations for our apartment. I didn't mind it at the time. What we had was still far better than where I came from, so I was happy. The only sad thing was I did not have my parents or the rest of my sisters and brothers to share this special time with. There were a few times during those long cold winter nights where I cried myself to sleep wishing my parents were with me. It was a very lonely time for me. In Vietnam, my mom would take me everywhere she went. I would never leave her side. Often times, my sister would tell me I was my mom's favorite. I would always get what I wanted. At the time, all I wanted was my mother there with me. But I would have to wait. Christmas came and went and the next thing I knew it was spring.

The rest of my fourth grade year went by pretty fast as I tried to absorb my new language and culture as fast and as much as I could. I remembered there were times when my sister and I were out in public and she tried to speak to me in Vietnamese, and I would ask her to speak to me in English only. My own reasoning for this at the time was the Vietnam conflict was still pretty fresh on people's minds, and some folks still harbored ill fillings toward the Vietnamese refugees living in America. So with that in mind, I did not want anyone to know we were from Vietnam just in case we came across those types of people who didn't like us.

My fifth-grade year was spent at Meadow Heights Elementary School. Beresford School closed down at the end of my fourth grade year, so they transferred all of us to the new school. Craig and I became better friends at Meadow Heights. I didn't know what it was, but I was learning English at a phenomenal rate. By my second year here, I was almost speaking English fluently. I was talking to everyone and sparing no one. I was very talkative, and that sometimes got me into trouble at school. Teachers would get upset with me when I talked too much during their teaching time. I would get sent to the office often. My grades also suffered because of my trying to be so social.

But the one area where I would excel was in physical education classes. I was getting all A's in PE classes, but barely B's and C's in other classes.

As a matter of fact, I was at Meadow Heights when I had my first ever crush on a girl. Her name was Lavette. She was beautiful and spunky. She had wavy, dirty blonde hair and very nice brown eyes. She was also very flirtatious. All the boys I knew had a crush on her. One of them was Matt. As soon as he knew I had a crush on Lavette, he became my fiercest competitor to try to win her heart. She would always play us against each other. Matt and I were in the same third-period-class with Lavette. He and I would pass notes back and forth to Lavette in our class and also during breaks. At lunch, Matt and I would try to sit next to her and her "crew." She would always favor Matt over me because Matt's family was well-off, and I was just an immigrant wearing second or sometimes thirdhand clothing. Whenever I came near her and her crew, they would laugh and look the other way, but if Matt came around, they would smile and talk to him. However, I had no shame and kept trying to win her over. I tried for the entire school year to win her heart, but to no avail, so I gave up.

October came around pretty fast and before I knew it, my first Halloween in America had arrived. My aunt told me all about Halloween. She explained that all I would have to do was to walk around and knock on people's doors and say trick or treat and I would be rewarded with candy. Are you kidding me? Free candy and all I had to do was just say trick or treat. I was so excited and couldn't wait for the night to arrive fast enough. I loved candy and couldn't wait to sink my teeth into all these special treats.

My aunt took me to a nearby store the day before Halloween and bought me a Spiderman costume and mask. I got home, put it on, and stood in front of the mirror for about ten minutes before taking it off. I was checking myself out from the side view, the back view, and of course the all-round view to ensure I was going to look good for that night. Then Halloween arrived. My aunt came by and picked us up around 7:00 p.m. that night. At first, I thought we would just go to walk around our neighborhood, but my aunt told us it was too dangerous, and besides the candy we would receive was not very good. She told us she was taking us up to the rich area where we would get a lot of good candies, and the area was much safer. I didn't care. I just wanted to get lots of candies. We arrived in the Hillsdale area. The area actually was very near my elementary school. I went right into action. I went up to the first house and rang the doorbell. A very nice lady opened the door, and I told her trick or treat. She gave me a big smile and complimented me on my Spiderman costume.

BRIAN HUYNH TRAVIS

That night, I went to as many doors as I could and must have said trick or treat almost a hundred times. By the time we got home that night, I was really tired, but my candy bag was enormous. I was so happy, I went through every piece of candy that was in that bag and broke them down into smaller piles. I had my favorite piles and not-so-favorite piles. Either way, I kept everything that was given to me on this special night and ate them for snacks for the next few weeks.

As we neared the end of our fifth-grade year, I learned that most of us would be attending Abbott Middle School, which was about three miles away from Meadow Heights. I also learned that Craig would be attending Turnbull Middle School near the Martin Luther King Jr. Center instead of going with us to Abbott. I was sad to see him go to a different school, but most of the group Craig hung out with was going with me to Abbott, so it was somewhat of a consolation. The summertime came and I didn't have anything to do except to hang out around the neighborhood. I often went to the Martin Luther King Jr. Center to hang out and play games. This was a great way to keep me out of trouble and also help me learn social skills and make new friends. At the same time, my sister started dating a Caucasian guy named Ron. He was tall and had blond hair. I came home one afternoon from the King Center and saw Ron in our apartment. My sister introduced him to me. He shook my hand and said hello. He appeared to be a nice guy. My sister told me he wanted to take us all out for ice cream. I was excited. We walked downstairs and got in his red Ford Pinto. He took us to Baskin-Robbins in downtown San Mateo and bought me a couple scoops of vanilla ice cream. That was the first time I met Ron. He dated my sister for a year or so before she let him go and began dating a Vietnamese guy.

By now, I was too busy with my life that I did not even care what was going on in my sister's and brother's lives. I was always hanging out with friends around the King Center or around the neighborhood. My sister was driving now, and at the end of that summer, she took me to the store and bought me some school clothes and school supplies. Then the day came when I had to go to Abbott for our first day. I was now a sixth grader. I went to the same bus stop near the King Center and waited for the yellow bus to come.

When we arrived at Abbott, I met some of my friends and spoke to them prior to the first bell. We went up to the board where they had all of our classes posted. While I was standing there, I looked down the hallway and guess who I saw. It was Lavette, my big crush from Meadow Heights. She was walking our way. Her hair was now curly, and she looked absolutely stunning. When our eyes met, she gave me a big smile. I told myself I was going to make my move as soon as she walked up to me. But then Matt stepped in the way and began talking to her. What a player hater! I was so upset. I was going to go up to her and pull her away from Matt. However, before I could do that, the first bell rang, meaning we had just three minutes to get to our classes before the tardy bell rang. I walked away pissed off at Matt. He gave me this look as if to tell me I got you again.

I went to my class hoping Lavette would be in one of my classes, but unfortunately she was not. I looked for her at lunch time, but I did not see her. What I did see and experience was something out of this world for me at the time. I accidentally bumped into an eighth grader by the name of Eric in the cafeteria. I said sorry, but apparently that was not good enough for him. Eric was a big white kid and appeared to be one of those that liked to pick on younger students. Just right after I said sorry, he said something to the effect of, "Watch where you are going, you, dumb Chinaman." I was in shock and just numb. I froze for a moment because I did not know what to do since this was the first time I have been in this country that I had experienced racism to this extent. There was another incident similar to it that happened that same morning, but it was not quite as extreme as this one.

I was sitting next to a girl in my fourth-period class, just right before the lunch period, when she coughed. I was paying attention to what the teacher was saying at the time, so I couldn't really tell if she had sneezed or not. So I said, "God bless you." I was just trying to be nice and polite. So, instead of correcting me that she had just merely coughed, she turned to me and said, "I just coughed, you stupid immigrant. You only say God bless you to someone who had just sneezed, so get it right." I thought to myself; wow that really hurt my feelings. I was just trying to be nice. I was hurt and embarrassed because others around me were now staring at me. I just turned and looked away.

So back to this little pickle I was in. I thought to myself there was no way I was going to let someone else pick on me because of the way I looked or acted. My fist became clenched, and I was ready to fight this guy. I did not care that he was much bigger than me or that he was an eighth grader. I just wanted to knock him out because I was so mad. But I just wanted to give him the benefit of the doubt just in case he didn't really say what I thought I heard him say. So I asked him again, "What did you say?"

He definitely made it very clear to me that I needed to watch where I was going, "Chinaman." Then he asked if I wanted to do something about it. I was game at the time. I told him that I was going to kick his f-fing butt for calling me a "Chinaman." Since he was a lot bigger than me, I wanted to get the first punch in, but as I was getting ready to swing at him, a teacher walked up to us and asked us if there was a problem. Man, these teachers were always there at the right time and the right place to prevent me from getting into trouble, or in this case get my butt beat. We both looked at the teacher and told the teacher there was no problem at all. I went on my way and Eric went on his. I thought I was going to deal with Eric at some point during the school year, but he seemed to have left me alone after that incident.

Other than that one incident, my sixth-grade year went by very uneventfully. By now, I thought my English was pretty good, but I did not know at the time that the English I was learning was mostly from hanging out with my friends at the King Center and around my neighborhood. One day, my aunt came by our apartment to see how we were doing and spoke to me about my school. I engaged in a lengthy conversation with her about it. After the conversation, she told me I was talking "Ghetto." I disagreed with her and thought I was speaking just fine. I told her that my friends in the neighborhood were helping me with English. She just shook her head and walked away. I didn't really care how I was learning English as long as I was learning, so I didn't really care about her opinion.

My sister and parents had been keeping in touch with each other via letters. But my parents stopped writing to us for a three-to-four-month period. The period was around the end of the 1981, which was the end of my sixth-grade year. We were concerned and did not know what was going on. Back in the early 1980's, mail was the only way to keep in contact with each other from halfway across the world. When we stopped receiving mail from our parents, we became very concerned. However, there was nothing we could really do at the time except to wait it out. We started writing to our remaining four sisters to see if our parents were okay. Then one day, we received a letter from our parents stating that they had also escaped from Vietnam by boat and that they were at a refugee camp in Malaysia. We were so happy. We were even happier when we heard two of our nephews were with them. My parents went through the same immigration process in order to be accepted to the United States. I was very happy to hear that my parents had successfully escaped, but after a few days I had completely forgotten about them and continued on with hanging out with my friends at the King Center. I guess I was being a typical kid at that point. Didn't really care about much except to play and go to school.

Six or seven months later, my sister told me that my parents would be arriving in the United States in a month. Again, I was ecstatic for a day or two, but then I would go back to what I was doing and not even think about them. I know I was so bad. Then the day came when we went to Travis Air Force Base in Fairfield to pick them up. I was excited and nervous at the same time. I was excited because I love and missed my parents very much, but I was also nervous because now I would have to follow my parents' rules. At this point, I was pretty much independent. Of course, I listened to my sister and brother and followed their rules, but I was used to their rules, and they were actually very lenient. It was the unknown that was making me nervous. I just told myself to expect the worse, as I couldn't hang out at the King Center anymore or roam San Mateo.

We arrived at Travis Air Force Base in the late morning. Just being there brought back great memories of me kissing the tarmac three years earlier when I first arrived in this country. How ironic was that. First it was me, my brother, and my sister arriving at Travis; then my parents and my two nephews. Travis Air Force Base was like our gateway to the West. I love this country. After they cleared customs, we all embraced and cried in joy. We were just so happy to be reunited with our parents. I was the youngest of eight and a mama's boy. My mom was so happy that you could not get that smile off her face for at least a week. We took them home to our apartment and got them situated. My nephews' names were Phan Ton Ngiem and Tuan Tran. We knew that we would have to look for a bigger place now that there were seven of us. There was no way we could all stay in that small two-bedroom apartment together. The next few days, my sister took my parents to the welfare office and registered for benefits. My sister also enrolled them in English classes at the Adult Day School so that they could assimilate sooner.

We started looking for a bigger place to move to. I was hoping we could find a house somewhere near Abbott School so that I could just walk to school instead of taking the embarrassing yellow bus to school every day. Who was I kidding? We were receiving welfare, so how could we afford to live up in the hills of San Mateo? There was no way we could afford to rent a house or even an apartment up there. The rent for a house in that area at the time was almost as much as the seven of us were receiving from welfare, but it was nice to dream though. This was the period when I was starting to really notice most, if not all, of my friends were rich and we were poor. Most of them were wearing Guess jeans and other designer clothing while I was wearing clothes from the Salvation Army Stores. I started to get embarrassed showing my lunch card at lunch time in front of pretty girls. And when I did use my free lunch card, it seemed the girls would whisper to themselves and then laugh and that made

BRIAN HUYNH TRAVIS

me feel really bad. I know I should have been grateful just to have a free lunch, but this was me at the age of twelve.

A few weeks later while the search for a bigger place was still going on, my sister dropped the bomb on me. She told us the guy she was dating had just bought a house in San Jose and he wanted us all to move down there with him. He was Vietnamese and appeared to be a nice guy. He was also a few years older than my sister. He sold my sister on the fact that San Jose has a huge Vietnamese population and we would fit in better down there. She was in love at the time, and she thought moving in with him and also being in an area where there were a lot of Vietnamese would actually help us assimilate faster.

Of course, I was very reluctant to go after my sister told us about the guy's proposal. I didn't want to leave all the friends I just made and the area I was now very familiar with. But my parents chimed in and said they would be better off being around the Vietnamese community since they were a little older and this would help them fit in more. I voiced my opinion and was loud about my objections to going. My father told me to be quiet, but I defied his orders and continued to talk. I wasn't talking back to him but just wanted to make sure my objection was being heard. This was the American culture in me that was coming out, because I would have never done this in Vietnam. In Vietnam, it was very acceptable to hit your children when they misbehave. There were no laws that made it a crime for a parent to spank their kids with belts, 2 × 4's, sticks, fists, etc. If I had still been there, my father would have grabbed his belt and spanked me with it already. But here, he allowed me to go a little further than he normally would. In the end, he told me to go lie down on the couch and wait for him while he went and got a belt from his pants.

He returned with his belt and began spanking me with it. He must have struck me on my buttocks and the back of my thighs at least six times with it. Boy, did it hurt really bad. I forgot how painful it was to get spanked with a belt. It had been a long time since I was spanked, but it definitely brought back memories real quick. Later that day when I went to go take a shower, I saw at least three belt marks on the back of my thighs. I never told anyone of my spanking or when my father used a long piece of wood to hit me because I had spoken back to him.

In the end, we were moving, and I really had no say in it. In the Vietnamese culture, it was not uncommon for you to still be living with your parents when you are in your twenties or thirties. Actually, it would be rude or ungrateful if you didn't take in your parents when they were old or needed your help.

We strongly believe in the family unit, so that was all the reason for my now-twenty-four-year-old sister to still be living with us at the time.

So we moved into this guy's house somewhere on Valley Haven Street in San Jose. I was to attend Davis Middle School. It was a three-bedroom two-bath house, but there were many of us at the time. My mom and my dad had their own room. My sister and her boyfriend had their own room. So, I shared a room with my brother and our two nephews. It was really tight in my room, so sometimes, I would sleep on the couch.

Binh's boyfriend was an engineer at some company in San Jose, so he was making good money. He had a big color television in the living room and other fancy stereo equipment around the house. My parents got to go to Vietnamese stores and restaurants nearby. Life was not bad at the time.

I was a seventh grader attending Davis Middle School. I participated in their after-school soccer and track programs. I was pretty fast on the soccer field and quick in track. My new friends started to call me the "Riceman." At first, I was like what was up with this nickname. I thought it had some racial overtone to it, so I confronted my friends who gave me the nickname. They reassured me it was a name of endearment because of my quickness and also because I was Asian. At first, that didn't make sense, but after a while, I didn't seem to care anymore. So I was known as the "Riceman" from that point onward at Davis Middle School.

Shortly after moving in, I befriended my neighbors across the street. They had two girls about my age, and they both went to my school. The younger one was in sixth grade, and the older one was in eighth grade. The older one's name was Paula. She was very flirtatious. After school, I would come over to her house and play around. Her parents were always at work until after 5:00 p.m., so I would stay there until they came home from work. When we played, she would always grab me and throw me on the ground. She liked wrestling with me and would always end up on top trying to pin me down. I thought it was strange, but hey, I was a boy. I went right along with it. I would pretend to fight back, but in the end I would always let her win. We had a great time, all the time. One day while she was sitting on top of me, she leaned down and put her lips on mine. I had never kissed a girl before this moment, so I did not know what to do. She told me to relax and gave me a long kiss. It was my first-ever kiss with a girl. We would continue to be very playful the entire time I lived across the street from her.

We would take our parents to the Vietnamese shopping centers so that they could mingle and make new friends. We loved eating pho at the Pho Saigon

Restaurant right off Tully Road. Pho is a noodle soup with thinly sliced beef mixed in with white noodle and other yummy ingredients. I used to have at least a bowl once a month. My seventh and eighth-grade years went right by me in a blink of an eye. I guess the old saying is right: "Time flies when you are having fun." I was looking forward to attending Oak Grove High School after the summer of my eighth-grade year. I felt pretty good about the new friends I had just made. I thought I would never have to move anywhere else again. Everything appeared to be going my way. The Oak Grove High School junior varsity football coach had met me at one of my track meets and told me he would love for me to play for his team. I was so excited and was looking forward to playing some football. But then, Binh developed feelings for a guy she had run into by chance who she used to know way back in Vietnam. They started to secretly see each other. I didn't know about this new guy and the implications this new romance would have for me in the near future until one summer night.

I found out about this the hard way when I heard Binh and her current boyfriend arguing loudly in the kitchen. He accused her of cheating on him and a whole bunch of other things. At some point during the argument, I thought the guy was going to hit my sister, so I ran into the kitchen with a stick and warned him to not even think about it. He looked at me crazy as if to say boy, I could kill you with my bare hands right now if I wanted to. My sister told me it was okay and that I needed to give them some privacy. So I retreated to my room. I stood by my door and listened intently as they continued to argue. Luckily, their argument never escalated into physical violence. Soon after that, my sister told me and my family that we were moving back to San Mateo. She apologized for placing us in this situation, but she had just broken up with her current boyfriend. He said we had to move out as soon as possible.

I was so disappointed and upset that I would have to move again. This was the second time after trying so hard to make new friends. As an immigrant and a poor person, it was hard to find good friends that would like you for who you were instead of what your parents had. This is how high school was back then, and I am sure that is the way it still is. If your friends think you have money, they will become friends with you, but if they know you are poor based on the way you are dressed or by word of mouth, they tend to be less approachable. That is just how life is.

So we all moved back to San Mateo and were living near the King Center again. It was now the summer of 1984. It was during this time that my sister and my brother parted ways. My sister went and lived with her new boyfriend, and my brother moved out to live on his own. That left me, my father, my mother, and my two nephews living together. We moved into a friend of my parents' house on South Claremont Street. The house was very small. My father and mother had their own room. I turned the entryway into a room, and my two nephews slept on the couch.

My parents were attending the Adult Day School in San Mateo again. They wanted to find work and get off government-assisted financial aid. That fall I began attending Hillsdale High School. Hillsdale was located in the hills of San Mateo. It was close to Abbott School, which I attended during my sixth-grade year. I would take the same yellow bus from in front of the King Center to Hillsdale every morning for school. Hillsdale had a student body of approximately sixteen hundred students, and over 90 percent of the students were white. There were approximately thirty of us on the yellow bus and we were all different ethnicities.

I was a little nervous and apprehensive about going to Hillsdale at first. I was not looking forward to trying to make new friends again or to reconnect with my old friends from Abbott. Then the day came when I arrived at Hillsdale as a brand-new freshman. I got off the yellow bus and looked at this enormous school. I was in awe. There were so many people walking around and there were cars parked everywhere. These cars weren't old clunkers either. These are really nice-looking cars. It was really overwhelming for me at the time. I walked around trying to find my old friends from Abbott. Luckily, I ran into a couple of them, and they made me feel a little bit better. We found our classes that were posted on the attendance office window. Before I knew it, the first few days of high school flew by.

I started to hang out with the friends I had from Abbott. There was Jeff C., Tim, Noel, Robert, Gary, and Frank. We would hang out together in the morning before class, at lunch time, and sometime after school at Tim's or Gary's house. We were the best of friends. These new feelings of friendship were new to me. In middle school, I was never close to Craig or my other friends, so I liked the new sense of camaraderie this new group generated. Tim, Jeff C., and I became the best of friends later on that year. Sometimes, I would spend a lot of time hanging out at Tim's house in the San Mateo village. At first, my parents did not want me to spend so much time at Tim's house. They soon realized he was a good kid and did not mind as much. My fear of my parents being really strict with me had quickly vanished. My mom was pretty easy on me with her rules. As long as I listened to her and was home at a certain time, I was free to hang out with my friends. My mom was the greatest.

BRIAN HUYNH TRAVIS

I went out for the junior varsity football team and made the squad. I was one of the fastest guys on the team. The other really fast player was Bryan. It was really exciting to be part of a team. Though the coach was really hard on us, all that hard work paid off in the years to come. The coach put me at wide receiver on offense and at defensive back on defense. The coach put Bryan at running back on offense and at the other defensive back position on defense. The coach told us he wanted to have quickness on both the offensive and defensive sides to have a chance to win games. Soon, Bryan and I were on the kickoff team returning kickoffs, punt teams returning punts, the hands team, and any other position available. Bryan and I never left the football field. Bryan and I didn't care. We loved it. We just wanted to start on this football team. I was given a team jersey and a number. The number on my jersey was 15.

Being a starter on the football team and the benefits that came with it didn't really hit me until our first pep rally prior to our first game. We were introduced by the spirit squad and our cheerleaders to the rest of the school during a lunch time rally. All the students were there, clapping and cheering. It was very exciting. I felt like a big shot now. Unfortunately, we lost our first game. We played lousy and were held scoreless by another school. I made one lousy catch on offense and had some tackles on defense. But overall, I played just as bad as my teammates. It's a team sport. Win or lose, we took credit together or the blame together. We were a team!

I tried to get my parents, brother, and sister to come watch my games, but they kept telling me they did not understand the game and didn't want to go. That made me a little sad knowing that other parents were out there cheering and supporting their kids and mine wouldn't even show up. But I got over it really fast. I started to notice that girls at my school were paying a little more attention to me now. They were friendlier to me now than before. It seemed that the girls didn't care or stare as much anymore when I came off that yellow bus every morning now. They wanted to be friends with a starter on the football team regardless of my being poor or an immigrant from Vietnam. I was now one of the cool dudes at our school. My one big crush from Meadow Heights, Lavette, was also at Hillsdale. However, she was no longer the big fish in a small pond. She was now a small fish in a big pond. There were so many other good-looking girls at Hillsdale.

I didn't pay attention to her anymore. Even Matt stopped chasing after Lavette. I started talking to a girl named Lennon. She was beautiful. She had blonde hair, light-brown eyes and was just really sweet. She and her friends, Debbie and Katie, started hanging out with our group. Our football season came to an end. I scored five touchdowns during the season. My overall quickness and versatility really impressed the varsity coach, Rich. Our junior varsity football team ended up with a 4-4 record for that year. Before I knew, the Grid came. The Grid was the pre-Christmas formal dance and the Prom was the end-of-the-year dance. I really wanted to take Lennon to the Grid dance, but my mom just didn't have any money to give me. The ticket alone would have made our family broke. Plus I didn't have money to rent a tuxedo and pay for our dinner that night. Lennon's parents were divorced, so she was living alone with her mother. They did not have any money either. So Lennon and I ended up not going. We would spend time at Tim's house or at Katie's house.

Then during our Christmas vacation, we were all hanging out at Katie's house. Katie's parents went away for the weekend, so she had a party at her house. During the party, she brought out alcohol from her parents' alcohol cabinet and began serving us drinks. That was the first time I actually drank alcohol. I remembered she poured all of us shots of Jack Daniels. We all drank the shots. I had only one shot that night, but I felt it right away. I was feeling funny at first, like someone had spun me round and round for five straight minutes. The room was spinning. Everyone else continued to drink more Jack Daniels and the house became very loud. We were all hanging out in her family room at the time.

Things were going really well for Lennon and me until she gave me bad news at the end of our school year. She told me that she and her mom were moving to Puerto Rico in the summer and she did not know if she was ever going to see me again. I was devastated by the news, but what was I going to do? Go with her? That was not in the cards for me, so that summer was a hard one for me. The only good thing I had going for me was Coach Mazzoncini had invited me to play on his varsity team. This was a big deal for sophomores. It was very seldom that a sophomore gets invited to play on a varsity team in high school. I felt very privileged and honored that he had invited me to play for him. He told me to report to the two-a-day practice in early August to prepare for the upcoming football season. I stopped dwelling over the loss of Lennon and started concentrating on playing football.

I took the bus to Hillsdale and arrived at our first practice. I was not surprised to see Bryan and another very good football player, Albert at the practice. We were the only three sophomores that were invited to play on the varsity team. As Bryan, Albert, and I sat there and waited for practice to start, we saw some of the seniors pull up in their cars. Others were driven there by their girlfriends. We were very envious of what we were seeing, and we told each other that we couldn't wait for our day to come in two years when we would finally be seniors.

That day we received our practice gear, helmets, and the blue practice jerseys. Our school name was the Knights and our school colors were red, white, and blue. How fitting that was. We assembled on the field and began our first practice of the summer. I noticed there were at least sixty to seventy players there that day. The racial makeup of the team was something like this: there were three to four Asians, three to four African Americans, two to three Hispanics, and the rest were Caucasians. As I was standing in the back of the formation, I was really intimidated by the fact that most of the guys in front of me were twice my size and that they were upper classmen. There are always stories about how seniors rule the school and what they say goes. I was only 5'10" and 150 pounds wet. I bit on my mouthpiece pretty hard to try to ease my fear and anxiety of being only one of three sophomores on the team. Having Bryan and Albert there helped ease my fear a little bit.

Coach Mazzoncini broke down the team into smaller groups. He began calling out names. I heard my name being called to go with the wide receiver group. Coach Brown was our wide receiver coach. There must have been twenty of us in this group. I was how would it be possible for me to start on this team with so many people vying for two starting spots. He had a senior go over the routes we would learn and run during practice. There were only ten routes, so they were not hard to remember. We learned the routes and ran them to perfection. The morning session was over, and we were giving an hour for lunch. I brought a sandwich and a drink for lunch. I ate lunch with Bryan and Albert. Then the afternoon session began with us being broken down into defensive groups. I was in the defensive back group with Bryan. We began practice by learning the fundamentals of footwork such as how to backpedal, how to break toward the ball, how to tackle, etc.

The coaches really worked us hard that day. There were a few times that day when some upper classmen tried to intimidate me by whispering to me that they were going to hurt me. I was afraid, but I remembered what Craig had told me about appearing weak. So I told them to bring it on. I made sure I remembered the people that tried to intimidate me and gave them that extra oomph when I went up against them during hitting drills. Craig was right again. Soon, they stopped trying to intimidate me and left me alone. I arrived home that night starving and aching everywhere. I told my parents all about football and how my first practice went. They paid very little attention to my story. My father did ask me why I wasn't playing soccer instead of the often violent football. I just told him there wasn't enough contact in soccer for me. I told him I loved hitting people on defense and scoring touchdowns on offensive. He gave up trying to convince me to play soccer and just smiled. My mother would always tell me to be careful on the football field and try not to get hurt.

Soon our two-a-day-practice sessions were over and that also marked the end of a very tired summer. Bryan and I again proved that we were two of the fastest guys on the team, so Coach Mazzoncini told us we would play a lot in the upcoming season. We were very excited. Just the thought of playing on the varsity team as a sophomore was awesome. To be playing a lot was a dream come true. We were giving our jerseys and my number was 8. I couldn't be any happier. I was now ready to take on my sophomore year with a lot of pride.

I asked my mother if she could buy me some new clothes from Macy's instead of Kmart. I specifically asked for Guess jeans and other popular brands. She told me Macy's was really expensive, but after begging her for hours she agreed to take me there and see if we could afford any. I was so happy that she even agreed to go with me. We took the bus to the Macy's store at the Hillsdale Shopping Center. We arrived and went straight to the boys section. We picked up a pair of Guess jeans and noticed it was about $50. "Wow, $50?" she asked. There was no way we could afford that being on welfare. We went to the shirt section and everything was well above what we could afford. I was disappointed but understood our financial situation. My parents were a little older than most refugees and plus they were learning English at a very slow rate. That did not help their quest to get employment. My mother went to some interviews, but the potential employers could not understand her very well, so none of them ever called her back. My dad was closing in on the retiring age, so he was also having a hard time finding a job.

My mother and I took the bus to Kmart on the way home, and she bought me some Wrangler jeans for about $12 each instead. We also picked up a few new shirts and some new underwear. She also had to buy new clothes for my two nephews that were living with us at the time. I love my two nephews dearly. They were like brothers to me. I wish I could have done more to help them ease into their assimilation process better. I should have done more to help my parents also. My sister and brother did a good job of helping them, but I should have helped too. By this time, I was too busy playing football and hanging out with friends. Our football season began on a good note. We played our first game against the South San Francisco High Warriors in South San Francisco. It was a night game. It was really exciting. I have never played before a big crowd before, let alone a night game.

BRIAN HUYNH TRAVIS

We arrived at the stadium and went into the visitor's locker room to go over some last-minute game plans. Then the moment of truth arrived. We were told to take the field. My heart now was pounding so hard that I could feel each beat. We walked to the edge of the stadium before Coach Mazzoncini led the charge onto the actual field. I looked around and saw so many people in both stands. It was an awesome feeling. South San Francisco won the coin toss and elected to receive the ball first. Coach Mazzoncini told me I was going to get some playing time at the right cornerback position. I was nervous, anxious, but at the same time I was ready to get it on.

I watched the entire first quarter on the sideline as we battled back and forth against a very tough South San Francisco team. At the end of the first quarter, Coach Mazzoncini motioned for me to come over to where he was. I had a feeling this would be the moment where I would be inserted into the game. Sure enough, he told me to get in there and play defense. I was really excited. I put my helmet on and placed my mouthpiece inside my mouth. I readjusted my elbow pads and checked to make sure my jersey was tucked in before running onto the field and into our defensive huddle for my first play on defense at the varsity level. That first play on defense would be the most memorable one during my high school football career. I remembered dropping back in the three-man-zone coverage when I saw their running back break through our defensive line. I looked closer and thought he was more like a lineman than a running back. The guy was either Tongan or Samoan, but his nationality was the least of my concern at the time. It was his size and speed that worried me the most. He was about 6'2", probably weight about 250 pounds, and he was rumbling my way! I was the only one between him and the end zone. I thought I was not going to survive this collision with him, but what was I going to do? Pretend to trip and fall and look like a coward? Or bite on my mouthpiece a little harder and go head-on with him and spend the next few days in the hospital? I really didn't like the latter, but I definitely did not want to be a coward at all. I bit on my mouthpiece as hard as I could and went straight for him. As I got closer, I began to lower my shoulder pads and prepare for the violent collision that was about to take place. I saw him lowering his shoulder pads also. I started to ask God to give me the strength I needed to take on this challenge. The next thing I knew I was on my back and staring at the stadium lights. The South San Francisco crowd roared as he scored the touchdown. I checked myself and realized I still had all my limbs and nothing was broken. Thank God! The Lord heard my prayer in time and protected me from the heavy impact. The guy just ran me over as if I was merely a speed bump. At least, it didn't hurt as much as I thought.

I got right back up and went to the sideline to await the eventual kickoff from their side. Coach Mazzoncini walked over and told me he was proud that I didn't back down from that big running back. That was that running back's only big run against us that night. Our defense played really well the rest of the game and we won that hard-fought battle. I played the entire second and fourth quarters at the defensive back position for the game. I made a few tackles on defense. I also made a nice catch on offense for a long gain.

The season went by really fast. We ended up being a 5-5 team that year. Bryan, Albert, and I played really well during the season and our stocks went up again with the coaching staff. They loved us and told us they were looking forward to next season. Coach Mazzoncini told me to join the track team in the spring so that I could increase my speed and stamina for my junior year. Of course, I agreed.

The football season was very busy with afterschool practices and game-day activities. My being able to spend time and hang out with Tim, Jeff, and the rest of our crew was affected by this. They would always ask me to do things after school and I would tell them I was busy. I started to split from the group. I had made new friends from the football team. I started to hang around with Bryan more and more. We would hang out at his apartment in Redwood City. His mother and sister really liked me. They were very nice folks. We would play the Atari game system at his apartment or just hang out and talk about football.

Bryan and I also loved to play basketball at lunch time during school. We used to grab a quick bite, run to our big gym, and play pickup basketball with others. One day, we were playing against some seniors. Jeff H. was one of the seniors. The goal was whichever team got ten baskets first would win the game and continue to play. The losing team would have to wait their turn to play again, so it was very competitive because no one wanted to wait. I was known as the "jumper" because I can jump really high to grab rebounds. Bryan was our shooter. Though the seniors were bigger than us, they were a little slower too. Bryan was running circles around these guys and I was grabbing every rebound on the board. This was making the seniors really mad. We were up 7-1. I fouled Jeff H. while trying to get a rebound over him. Right after I fouled him, he said, "You stupid Chinaman. Quit fouling me or I will beat your ass." There is no other word in the English language that would get me more upset than calling me a "Chinaman." Even though I was a Vietnamese, in some people's eyes, it did not matter what your nationality was. As long as you were Asian, you were considered a "Chinaman."

I asked Jeff H. to apologize to me for calling me "Chinaman." He laughed out loud and began cursing at me as if I was the one who said something that had offended him. Then he got in my face and pushed my chest with both of his hands. I stumbled backwards but quickly regained my balance. Before I could tell him not to touch me again, Jeff H. started walking up to me in a very aggressive manner. It seemed as if he was either going to push me again or attempt to hit me. As he got closer, I had no choice but to try and defend myself. I unleashed the biggest roundhouse I could generate. I struck him on the left side of his face, knocking him straight to the ground. Bryan and some other people quickly grabbed me and pulled me away. I ran out of the gym as fast as I could because I did not want to get into trouble. Though I did not start the fight, our school policy was it did not matter who started the fight. Whoever was involved would be suspended or possibly expelled from school and that was something I did not need. My parents would have killed me. Later that day, I saw Jeff H. walking down the hallway. I noticed the left side of his face was a little swollen and red. He looked at me and I looked back at him. That was the extent of that encounter. We went our separate ways and nothing was brought up about that incident again.

My popularity had grown. Bryan and I were the talk of our class because of our successes on the football field. By now, I was hanging out with Bryan and the rest of the "jocks" at lunch time. Bryan and I were the only two people that were from poor families living out of the Hillsdale area while the rest of our jock friends were from well-off families living close to the school. Our friends would share their lunches and also whatever snacks they had with us. I truly believe that if we weren't good in sports, none of the rich kids would allow us to hang around with them.

Our annual Grid was fast approaching. Everyone was trying to see who they would ask to the Grid. A couple of my friends asked me if I was going and who I would take. They wanted to know if Bryan and I would go with them as a group and rent a limousine. At first, it sounded like a lot of fun, but I really did not know if my mother could afford to pay for my ticket, let alone the limousine. Of course, there were other expenses that I hadn't taken into account at this time. I spoke to Bryan about it, and he too said he would have to check with his mother to see if they could afford it. I came home from school that afternoon and spoke to my mom about the possibility of me going. My dear mom gave me this look. She knew I really wanted to go. She paused for a moment and thought it over. Then she told me to find out how much everything would cost, and perhaps she could spare some money from our tight budget for me. I was so happy at the possibility of going to this dance that I gave her a big hug and a kiss. I immediately made some phone calls to my friends and got the prices within a few hours. From what I was able to find, the dance ticket was $50 × 2, tuxedo rental was approximately $75, splitting the limousine rental cost could run $100 each couple, dinner could cost each couple $50-$75, and a corsage for my date could run about $10. So when I added it all up, it was a mind-boggling $360. There was no way we could afford that kind of money for a dance. At the time as a whole family, we were receiving approximately $1,000 a month for food and rent (food stamps included.)

I was very disappointed but did not give up. I really wanted to go. This would be my first formal dance of any sort, so I was determined to make this work. I decided not to tell my mother what I had just learned from my friends. I wanted to wait until after I had spoken to Bryan and the other two friends at school the next morning before I told her. When I saw Bryan at school the next day, he had this disappointing look on his face. I knew right away he couldn't afford to go. Bryan and I saw our other two friends during the first break and broke the news to them. They were disappointed we could not all go together, but they said they understood.

Bryan and I spoke about it again at lunch, and we came up with some really good ideas. We thought about borrowing nice suits from our relatives instead of renting a tuxedo. That would cut $75 from our budget. We thought about asking my sister or his mother to drive us. That would cut an additional $100 off our budget. We also thought about just going to low budget restaurant for dinner instead of the somewhere fanciful. This should knock another $25 off our budget. Our new budget would just be around $160 instead $360. I got home that day and started on the tasks I needed to work on in order to make my plan work. First, I called my sister to see if she could drive us. I was really nice on the phone, so right away she knew I was up to something. She asked me, "Okay, what do you need, Hung?" I told her I really wanted to attend a formal dance and if she would drive me, my date and Bryan and his date. She was a little hesitant until I explained to her that this would be my first formal dance ever and how much it really means to me. She thought about it and agreed to drive us that night. I was really happy. I provided her with the date and time and she said she would see us then. I thanked her endlessly before hanging up.

My next step was to borrow a suit from my uncle Tom. I called him at his barbershop and told him that I was planning on attending a formal dance at my school and that I needed to borrow one of his suits. Instead of asking me more

BRIAN HUYNH TRAVIS

about the dance, he began laughing out loud. I didn't know what to think. I thought to myself at least he was laughing, even though it was at my expense. If it meant by the time he was done laughing that he was going to lend me one of his suits, so be it. Let him laugh all he wants. He laughed for a few seconds, though it felt longer than that. He then asked me mockingly who would be willing to go with me to the dance. I thought that was mean of him to say. I was a pretty handsome guy. I was 5'10" 150 lbs. I had an athletic build and a bowl haircut. I had a bowl haircut because my sister and mother used to cut my hair by sticking a bowl on my head and cutting around it. After my uncle got done poking fun at me, he said I could borrow one of his suits. He told me just to drop by his house sometime in the next few days and try them on. I thanked him for his help.

After I determined I could go to the Grid on a $160 budget, I approached my mother. I was really nervous that she would say no. I really wanted to go to this dance even though I hadn't found a date yet. I was thinking that finding a date would be a lot easier than having enough money to go. My mom was sitting in her room. I cautiously approached her and sat down right next to her. I gave her a big hug. Before I could say anything, she asked, "Well, so how much will it cost for you to go?" I told her about $160. She gave me this look like I was crazy because she thought it would be a lot less than that. Before she could say no, I explained all the expenses for the dance and the steps I took to alleviate half of it. I began to beg her again to allow me to go. She thought about it long and hard for a few moments and said, "All right, you can go, but I can't give you allowance for the next two months." I was so ecstatic. I agreed not to get any allowance for at least two months. My mom gave me $3 a week for helping her with the house chores.

I immediately called Bryan and told him I had been giving the green light to go. However, based on Bryan's voice over the phone, I knew Bryan would not be able to go with us. At the end of our conversation, he told me they did not have enough money for him to go to the dance. We were both very bummed out by this fact. I saw him the next morning at school and we spoke at length on how we could still try to get him to go. Without money for the ticket and dinner, chances of him going were slim to none. I was disappointed for him, but I still had to find a date so that I could go with my other friends. At the time, I liked a girl, named Christine. She was in one of my classes and we spoke during class and also in passing. She was really nice and very pretty. She was somewhat popular and usually hung around with her clique of girlfriends. They were all from well-off families. I was always very conscious of that. I just wanted to fit in. There were so many times when I would be envious of hearing my other friends inviting people over to hang out at their house. I wished I could have also invited friends over to my house, but where were they going to hang out? In my makeshift room that was really an entry hallway? I told myself I would have to make the best of what I had at the time.

I also told myself I was going to ask Christine to the dance. The worse thing she can do is say no. I really didn't have anything to lose. I also didn't want to ask her in front of her friends either. I wanted to ask her when she was alone. I had a feeling that her friends didn't really like me, because of who I was, where I came from, and also because of my family's financial situation or lack of it. Then I got a break. It was right before our third-period class when she and I arrived to our room a little bit early. She sat only a few seats away. There were a few other students inside the room with us at the time. I told myself this had to be the time for me to ask her, or I would not get this opportunity again. I decided I was going to do it. I felt my heart beating faster and harder by the second. I got up from my chair and walked up to her. I started out with the small talk but quickly transitioned into the intelligence collection phase. I ascertained if she was going to the dance and if she was who she was going with. I waited anxiously for her reply, hoping she would answer yes to my first question and no to my second. Thank goodness, those were her answers. I was quite happy for a quick second, and then I felt my heart was about to jump out of my chest as I posed the question to her, "Christine, will you go to the Grid with me?" Then there was dead silence.

I felt as if time had come to a standstill as I stood there awaiting her answer. She looked at me and looked at me. I was thinking to myself please say something. I thought I was about to have a heart attack if she didn't say something soon. My heart was beating so fast and very hard. I felt like I was going to sweat profusely. Then, she smiled and said, "Yes." She made me the happiest person at Hillsdale. I saw Bryan at lunch time and told him I had asked Christine to the dance and she said yes. At first, Bryan thought I was just kidding and did not believe me. When he saw her later that day, he asked her himself and sure enough she told him she had said yes to me. He was very happy for me, because Christine was not only very nice, but also popular with the students in our class. I'm pretty sure that some of her friends did not approve of the fact that she was going to the Grid with a poor immigrant from Vietnam, because their words got back to me through our mutual friends.

I didn't care what her friends thought about me, and quite frankly, I was happy that they felt that way. I was also happy Christine was not like some of her friends. I came home that night and went to my uncle's house to try on some of his suits. He asked me all sorts of questions about Christine. Who she was, if she was white or black, if she was rich or poor, if she was nice or not, and if her parents knew I was Vietnamese. I was thinking to myself I was just there, trying to borrow a suit and did not want to answer a million questions from him. However, at the same time, I did not want to piss my uncle off either. In the Vietnamese culture, the elders command your utmost respect and you best try not to offend them, or else things would go really bad for you. So I did my best to answer all his questions to the best of my ability without offending him. Thank God, he was satisfied with all my answers. He then walked me to his closet, and I went through all his suits to see which one would fit me the best. After a few hours, I was able to find a suit that fit me nicely. Since the Grid was a few weeks away, I told him I would pick it up then. My uncle agreed.

I would continue to talk to Christine in our third period class and also in passing. I purchased our tickets two weeks prior to the dance. I was counting the days down and hoping she would not cancel on me at the last minute. The day before the Grid, a friend of mine and his date offered to drive us. I spoke to Christine about it at lunch and she was okay with that. When I came home that afternoon, I called and thanked my sister, but told her she no longer had to drive us. She was happy with that. I went to my uncle's house and picked up the suit he was going to lend me. He had pressed it for me. I was very grateful for that. I went to the flower shop and bought a corsage for Christine. Everything was ready. All that awaited us now was for the day to arrive.

The day finally came. I got all dressed up in the nicely pressed suit. My mom said I looked very handsome. This was the fist time I had worn a suit of any kind, so I felt pretty important that night. My uncle had given me his leftover bottle of Polo cologne. I was very generous with the cologne on myself. I was looking good, feeling good and smelling good. I was thinking to myself I was ready for this big night. My friends came by and picked me up at about 5:00 p.m. From there, we drove to Christine's house which was located in the San Mateo Village.

We arrived and went to her front door. Her mother opened up the door and greeted us with a very friendly smile. After I introduced myself and our friends, she invited us inside. Her father was waiting for me inside. I did not hesitate to walk over and shake his hand. I just wanted him to know that his daughter was in good hands with me. I think he appreciated the gesture. But, boy, did he have a strong grip! I thought my hand was going to break by the way he was squeezing it. I got the feeling he wanted me to understand that if

I tried anything funny that night, I would have to pay for it. I definitely got his message with that handshake. I wasn't going to try anything funny that night anyway. Christine was a very respectable person, so the thought of trying anything funny with her never even crossed my mind. Her mother got the four of us together and took some photos. Her parents told me Christine had to be home before midnight. I told her that I would have Christine back way before then. The looked very happy to hear that. We left Christine's house and went out to dinner.

We went to an Italian restaurant near Hillsdale mall. I knew I had approximately $75 to spend on dinner. That was a lot to me at the time. I looked at the menu and saw the prices were not all that bad. It depended on what kind of an appetizer you considered ordering. The prices for these items ranged from $4 to $12 and a steak dinner was about $15. Plus a soda and some dessert would still come up well short of the $75 I had allotted for dinner. Of course, being stingy I didn't order any appetizers when it came to my turn to order and I got a glass of water instead of a soda. I was trying to make my mom proud by bringing back leftover money. It would show her that I was thrifty and always watching my money. I wanted to win some brownie points from my mom for future dances, like the Prom in May. I was always thinking ahead.

We had a very good dinner and I ended up only spending $50 for the both of us. That is unheard of nowadays. Back then, $50 could take you a long way. After dinner, we went to the dance. It was located at the old Dunfey Hotel in San Mateo. We arrived and met our other friends. Everyone was looking very good. People were arriving in stretch limos and other fine luxury cars. I didn't care. It would have been nice to arrive in a limo, but I was just happy to be there period. Christine and I ended up sitting with her group of friends and their dates. Luckily, I knew some of the guys in that group, so it wasn't all that bad. We ended up dancing most of the night. It was an awesome experience. I didn't want the night to end. This was the one night when I felt like I belonged. I didn't feel like an outsider or an immigrant just off the boat. I felt like an American. Everyone on the dance floor did not care who you were or what you were. We all just danced and had a good time that night. At the end of the night, we drove Christine home. We got to her house before midnight as promised. I walked her up to the door and told her I really had a good time. She said she had a great time. I was waiting for a good-night kiss. She then gave me a hug and a kiss on the cheek. I was good with that. I came home that night and told my mother all about the dance and how much I had saved from not splurging at dinner. My mother told me she was proud of me and I could

BRIAN HUYNH TRAVIS

have $5 of the $25 I brought back. That made a good night turn into a great night. I couldn't have asked for a better finish than that.

After the Grid, things went back to the way they were before with Christine hanging out with her clique. I went back to hanging out with Bryan and my other jock friends. The rest of the year went by pretty uneventful. I joined the track team and did really well in the field events and the 100-meter dash. I won a few medals at the end of the year at our league track championship. I dated a few other girls and had a great time, but nothing significant. I was really looking forward to my junior year because of football and track.

The beginning of my junior year, I began dating Dianne. She was beautiful with big brown eyes and light brown hair. She had a great sense of humor, but right away she told me her parents did not like people of color. At the time I did not really care. I loved her and was hoping I could change her parents' way of thinking if I could just meet and talk to them. I was a pretty funny guy and not a bad dude at all. However, I would never get the chance to meet her parents. She told me her parents would be furious with her if they knew she was dating a Vietnamese guy, so there was no way she was going to tell them about me. I was disappointed I would not get the opportunity to meet them, but what else could I do? My mother had scraped enough money together and bought me a used car so that I could drive to and from my school activities. I used to drop Dianne off after school, just right before football practice. I would drop her off a block away from the house and she would walk the rest of the way. That year, I did not go to the Grid or the Prom. I couldn't go with her, so I did not want to go with anyone else at all. Our relationship ended at the beginning of my senior year due to irrevocable differences.

My senior year went by in a flash. I was the co-captain of my football team and we finished the season 9-1. Unfortunately, we lost our playoff game to Terra Nova 6-14. I continued to be very successful in track and field. I usually won my long-jump and triple-jump events in our league meets. I placed in the top three in regional meets in the same events. I went to my senior Prom with my girlfriend, Katie. She was tall, beautiful and had a great personality. She was taller than me, so she had to wear flat-heeled shoes for our Prom pictures. Her mother did not have any issues with me because I was Vietnamese. Her mother actually liked me. We were a great couple until Katie and her mother had to move to Florida. It was sad to see Katie move, but there was nothing I could do except to thank her for the great memories. I began hanging out with Rey more and more towards the end of my senior year. We would always stop by the Lisa and Leslie house. Rey and I were really good friends with Lisa and Leslie. Their parents really loved us. They always fed us and made us feel really welcomed in their house. They were the best. Before I knew it, graduation arrived and my high-school years were over. Those four years were the best high school years I could ask for.

Becoming an American Citizen

SHORTLY AFTER GRADUATING from high school in 1988, I drove to San Jose to take an oral test about U.S. government and history and also demonstrate fluency in speaking and writing English in order to become an American citizen. There must have been hundreds of people of all nationalities standing in line, waiting to take the test. Though there were only ten questions for the oral test, there were one hundred questions and answers to study and choose from. Without proper preparation, even many U.S. born citizens would fail it. This was a gigantic obstacle for me. I studied for hours at a time in the days leading up to the test and I was able to pass the test with flying colors. I was so happy. I was filled with excitement and joy during the swearing in ceremony which had fifty other people who had passed the test. When prompted, we all stood up in groups when our country of origin was called. After everyone had stood up, we swore the Oath of Allegiance to our new country. We were now from "One Country." We were all fellow Americans. I was filled with American pride and a sense of civic pride as I realized I could now vote and make a difference as an active citizen in my adopted country. Before becoming a citizen of this great country, I felt like I did not have the right to comment on America's direction since I was considered an outsider. Now, I have a voice and a vote with which I would use to try to improve the quality of life here in my new country.

After the swearing in ceremony, I went to the clerk's office to finalize my court paperwork. The courtclerk asked me if I wanted to keep my original name. I had thought about this for a few weeks now. I knew I had a chance to change my name if I wanted to.

This was where the assimilation thing set in. I was thinking to myself I was about to become an American citizen for life. Why not change my first name to something that was American? I had done research on which American names would come close to the meaning of Hung, my Vietnamese name. Hung in Vietnamese meant brave and noble. I came across Brian which had similar meanings, so I chose Brian to replace Hung. Also, while growing up here, my friends couldn't pronounce Huynh, so for short, they gave me the nickname "Wynn." I told the court clerk my new name would be Brian Wynn Huynh. She assisted me in recording my new name for my naturalization certificate. This was what I had been working so hard for ever since I arrived here in 1979. I was looking forward to my first opportunity to vote. I was so proud to be an American.

At the same time, I did not really know what to do with my life now I could not get a scholarship to play football anywhere. I spent most of my time hanging out with Rey, Chris, Kimi, and Tim. We would play basketball during the day and drink beer at night. It was not a life that I wanted to lead, but at the time, I did not know what else to do. I had no clear goals and was undisciplined. There were weekends when we would crash parties and get drunk. Or we would hang out at the Shoreview Park with our Tongan friends.

We used to get into a lot of trouble around town while crashing other people's parties. Sometimes, we started trouble. Sometimes trouble just found us. I remembered at this one party near the Kehoe area in San Mateo, we were leaving because someone had called the police due to loud music. I was with Rey, Chris, Tim, and Kimi. They were walking ahead of me. As I was making my way out the side gate, I accidentally bumped into one of a group of guys from Foster City. They were all Caucasians. There were six or seven of them. I said sorry, but the guy became belligerent with me. By the time we got to the street, he had called me all kinds of names. The one that caught my attention was, "You are a fucking gook." I stopped and asked him what he called me and he said, "You are a fucking gook." I walked up to him and said, "A gook? Are you kidding me? These are fighting words to me if you don't apologize." Unfortunately, he had liquid courage (been drinking many beers) in him and refused to apologize. The next thing I knew he tried to swing at me. So I defended myself by ducking his wild swing and countered with a punch of my own, knocking him on the ground. Then all his friends tried to jump me, but little did they know Tim, Chris, Rey, and Kimi were with me. The next thing I knew we were fighting these guys. However, there was no contest. We ended up beating them all up before they ran back to their cars and took off. We were fortunate that this was a time period where we could still get into fights and not have to worry about getting shot or stabbed.

After the fight, I was just thinking about what, if I was there by myself. I would have gotten beaten up pretty bad or, even worse, be dead. This was because I was Asian and perhaps seemed to be a passive and weak person, an easy prey. I have read stories about how some young Vietnamese immigrants from other states were beaten up or killed because of their race. I had good friends around me and I never felt afraid of getting jumped or beaten up anywhere I went. Our group was very tight and we went everywhere together. There would be many more parties and many more fights by the time 1991 rolled around. In early March of that year, I started talking to Joy, a girl I had dated a short time in high school. We had kept in touch, but I never really pursued her seriously after our short relationship ended at Hillsdale. Our talks became very intense and long. We would spend some nights talking on the phone until the early morning hours. Sometimes, we would fall asleep on the phone together. We were deeply in love. She is just a beautiful person on the inside as well as the outside. She is Filipina with a little mix of Caucasian. She has dark brown hair and green eyes. She is tall. She has a wonderful heart and is very caring. She is just absolutely beautiful overall. Her parents caught on that we were seriously talking again and they did not like that very much. They did not want us to talk for many reasons. Some being that my parents were not rich, I was hanging out with people they deemed were losers and trouble makers, or I was not white.

I realized they only wanted the best for Joy, but at least they gave me a chance to prove that I was not a bad guy as they first thought. They would limit how much time she could spend talking to me on the phone each day. They would only allow Joy to go out with me one day a week. Joy was nineteen years old at this time, but because she was still living at home, she had to follow her parents' rules. Her parents made it very tough for us to see each other. However, we did not let them come between us. On March 15, I officially asked her to be my girlfriend. Luckily, she said, "Yes." I was very happy that day. Little did she and I know at the time that nineteen years later, we would still be together and with four beautiful daughters in our happy family.

After Joy and I started going out, she became pregnant with our first child, Briana. When Joy first told me she was pregnant, I did not know what to think. I was very happy about the fact that I was going to be a father, but I started thinking about other things that Joy and I would need in order to have a life together. I knew the one absolute thing I was going to do was I would marry her. Other than that, I had to figure out how I was going to support our new addition to our family. I later told my mother about Joy being pregnant. She was happy for me, but she too had the same concerns that I had. She told me I had to get my act together and get a real job—a job that would pay me enough to be able to support Joy and myself, plus our new baby. I told my mother and

Joy not to worry and that I was going to start looking for a good job. I was going to curb back on hanging out with the boys.

When Joy's parents found out she was pregnant, they became really mean to her. They refused to let her talk on the phone. They took away the keys to her car and told her she was not allowed to see me anymore. One day, Joy managed to get the phone away from her mother and called me to come and pick her up from her house. I came and got her and what little things she could take with her. We went back to my house. I was living with my mother on the 100 block of South Fremont Street in San Mateo. We did not have much there. We were renting the front of the house from another family. We had two very small front bedrooms, a small dining room, a small refrigerator, and a bathroom. We shared the kitchen with the other family. I had a small TV, a bed and a dresser in my room.

My mom and I were very happy to just have each other and a place to live. I was spoiled with my mom home cooked meals everyday. When Joy moved in, my mother began cooking meals for three. Joy loved her cooking too. Joy never had Vietnamese food before, so this was a real treat for her. Shortly after Joy moved in, I heard that my friend's father had an asbestos removal company that was looking to hire somebody. She told me the job would pay me somewhere around $12 an hour. As soon as I heard $12 an hour, I quickly seized the opportunity and told her I would love to work for her dad. She told me she would put in a good word for me. Back then, if you made $12 an hour without a college degree, then you were doing pretty good. Most jobs were offering between $5 and $10 an hour at the time for someone without a college degree. So I was really hoping I would get this job. The money I might make from this job would help me save for an apartment for Joy and I in the near future.

A week or two went by before I got the call. It was her older brother on the phone. He introduced himself as the manager for the asbestos removal company. He asked me to meet him at a coffee shop in Foster City the next day for an interview. I was really excited. I showed up at the coffee shop and had a really good interview with him. He told me he would call me the next day to let me know if I got the job or not. I came home that day and told Joy and my mom of how well I thought I did at the interview. They both hoped I would get the job.

The guy called me back and said I got the job and to report to the company headquarters in Union City the next day for orientation. I was so happy. I jumped for joy. I told my mom and Joy about the good news, and they too were happy for me. The next day I showed up in Union City and completed a bunch of paperwork in the morning. After I completed the paperwork, they assigned me to a crew. I was to work for the foreman, Jose and his partner, Francisco. They were funny folks. Jose and Francisco are from Mexico and they love to joke around. Right off, they said my nickname would be "Chino." They assured me it was not a racist Spanish word for Chinaman. I believed them and we went to our first job. I did not know much about asbestos work at the time except it could possibly be dangerous for your lungs if you breathe a lot of it in. Jose would always tell me that asbestos was fake, and it was another way the government was creating more jobs to help with the economy. We arrived at our first job somewhere in Hayward. We were supposed to remove some heating ducts around the furnace that had the asbestos tape wrapped around them. The furnace was located in the basement of this home. Jose told me to grab a roll of four-mil plastic from the van, three white disposable suits, plastic gloves, garbage bags, and three breathing masks. I came back with the equipment. He and Francisco showed me how to build a wall of plastic around the furnace and the asbestos heating ducts. After we built this enclosure, we put on our disposable suits, plastic gloves, and our breathing masks.

We then went inside the enclosure and began ripping the ducts down. I saw some dust floating in the air from us breaking off the ducts, but other than that, it did not seem too bad. We also had an air filtration system that was on at the time. After we got all the ducts down, we placed them in the garbage bags and put them in our van. We sprayed the area with some encapsulation chemical before leaving. Jose congratulated me afterward and said I had just completed my first asbestos removal job. He also told me that was what we would be doing most of the time, and the job was not all that hard. I was thinking to myself I could do this for a while before I find something else to do. I just couldn't see myself as a lifelong asbestos remover. I didn't want to bring that stuff home to my family just in case asbestos was really dangerous.

Joy's parents did not speak to her for the first month or so after she moved in with me, but they began reaching out to her. They told her they were willing to accept the fact that she was pregnant and she was dating me. They asked Joy and me to come live with them so that we could save our money. I told my mother about their request. I told my mother I would still help her with her rent. She said it was okay and that I needed to be with my wife. I know she was sad to see me leave. I was an adult now, but I was still her baby. She did not want to live alone. I knew this, so I visited and called my mother often to see how she was doing and just to talk to her.

My relationship with Joy's parents really improved over the years. They realized that I am actually a good guy, a hard worker, a good father, and a good son-in-law. They embraced me and accepted me. I have also embraced them and Joy and I are very grateful to them, Joe and Jeannette, for babysitting our children whenever we needed them.

BRIAN HUYNH TRAVIS

Joining the California Army National Guard

ON JULY 15, 1993, I went to the United States Army recruiter's office and enlisted in the Army National Guard. The reason why I enlisted was to give back to my country, my state, and the people who have given me and my family so much. I also wanted to obtain skills, discipline, and training from the greatest organization in the world.

With me that day was my good friend Huy. He also wanted to give back to this country for giving him and his family a chance to succeed in life. Huy and I went to the recruiting office on Humboldt Street in San Mateo, California, hoping to sign up to be combat medics. We wanted to use the medic skills and obtain a job in the civilian field. We were both a little nervous because we obviously have never committed to anything this serious before in our young lives. We realized that if we liked what we heard from the recruiter and the Army had combat medic slots for us, then we would agree to sign the contract. That was the other issue that Huy and I spoke about. We both did not want to commit to any four-year contracts because we did not want to be away from our families for that long. I don't think my mom or Joy would have liked for me to be gone for that long either.

My wife had also had just given birth to my first daughter, Briana, six months earlier. She too did not want me gone long nor did she want to move with me to my duty assignment once I completed my training. That left me with joining the Reserves. A friend of mine had recommended that I speak to a California Army National Guard recruiter to obtain further information about them. He told me that I would only have to attend drill once a month and training two weeks out of the year. Though I did not know much about the Guard, I did know from talking to my friend that I would not be regular Army.

We arrived at the armory and went to the recruiter's office. We spoke to the recruiter and told him our wishes were to join the Army National Guard as combat medics. He initially tried to talk us into joining regular army as infantrymen, but after we repeatedly turned down his recommendations, he agreed to help us explore the National Guard option. I think we were just a number to him as he tries to make his monthly recruiting goal. He told us a lot of neat things about the National Guard like how unlike any other service, the Guard serves a dual-role purpose. The first and foremost role is to the state in times of natural disasters, civic disturbances, and other duties. The second role is to the federal missions of overseas deployments. Guard units could be mobilized at any time with permission from the state's governor by the presidential order to supplement regular armed forces and upon declaration of a state of emergency by the governor of the state in which they serve.

He provided us with an example: our governor had blessed the California National Guard units to deploy to Operation Desert Shield in Kuwait in 1991 shortly after Iraq invaded that small country. He said by being in the Guard we could drill once a month and conduct annual training for two weeks a year. There was also the possibility to get called to active duty to conduct real-world missions and when that mission was over, we could go back to being part-timers again. He went on to explain that it was like having the best of both worlds. It sounded really good to us.

He scrolled through his desktop computer for a few minutes and then told us he had found two slots for combat medics with the HHSC 2/159 Infantry Battalion (Mechanized) in San Jose. We would have to attend basic training boot camp at Fort Sill, Oklahoma, on August 24, and then advanced individual training (AIT) at Fort Sam Houston, Texas, on October 12. However, in order to get to basic training on time, we had to depart on August 17. He continued on to tell us that after AIT, we would be finished with our training and return home and report to our National Guard unit sometime in February 1994. Huy and I looked at each other in agreement, knowing this was something we had wanted before walking into the armory. Before signing, we asked the recruiter what our rank would be if we signed that day. He told us we both would go in as privates, or PV1, because we didn't have a college degree. Otherwise, we could go in as a Private First Class (PFC) or even as a Specialist (SPC.) Right after the recruiter was done making his speech, we immediately agreed to sign the six-year California Army National Guard contracts and attend basic training in August. After we signed the contracts, we left the armory.

I remembered standing outside the armory parking lot on North Humboldt Street, looking at Huy and asking him, "Holy cow! What did we just do?" He looked back at me and calmly answered, "Well, this was what we wanted to do, so we are going for basic training in August." I shook his hand and did the manly hug and said, "All right, let's do this."

BRIAN HUYNH TRAVIS

I got home later and told my mom I had just signed up for the California Army National Guard. She told me she didn't want me to join the Guard, but if that was what I wanted to do, then she will support me. Asian parents usually want their children to grow up and become doctors, engineers, or lawyers. They do not want their children to join the Army or become police officers. The reasons for this would be: was prestige, bragging rights with other parents, and also monetary reasons. In Asia, most countries do not pay their soldiers very well and the training and living conditions were also bad. Police departments are concerned, they were often replete with corrupt cops, so parents did everything they could to prevent us from joining the force. My mom was not any different from any other Asian parent. She did what most parents would do, though, and that was to support their children even though I was joining the Army.

I also told my wife later that afternoon about my enlistment with the National Guard. She was very supportive of my decision since we had been talking about it for the last few weeks. She knew that I wanted to do well for our daughter and our future and the good intentions behind my enlistment. We were living with her parents in Foster City. They were helping us with caring for Briana since her and I both worked full time jobs. I felt comfortable knowing that if I were to leave for about six months to train in Oklahoma and Texas, Joy would have the support from her parents and family members with the caring of Briana while Joy went to work during the day.

For the next month, I tried to spend as much time as I could with Briana and the family before leaving for boot camp. I would come home from work and go straight to her. I loved picking her up and just hugging her. Even though the hugs might be just for seconds, they somehow cured everything that went wrong at work and brought me nothing but peace and tranquility while I was with her. It's funny how a child will change a person. It didn't really matter what you were doing or who you were. After having a child, you become this gentle father to the most beautiful and precious creation God has ever created. I thank the Lord every day for giving me Briana.

On August 10, 1993, Huy and I had an appointment at the Military Entrance Processing Station (MEPS) in Oakland. This is the place where new recruits get medically screened, complete the paperwork, and swear into duty. Huy and I met our recruiter at the armory in San Mateo, about 0500 hours. He then drove us to our appointment at 0700 hours. We checked in and were given a medical folder with a checklist to complete. There were over twelve medical stations we had to go through for that day. I remembered one of the stations where we had to get naked for a full physical examination. What was funny about this station wasn't the fact that we had to get naked, but having to stand naked while other new recruits were also present in the room. The male doctor stood behind the thin drape and called for us to come in one at the time. The doctor examined me pretty thoroughly. There were times where I was uncomfortable and I felt like he took a little bit longer than I expected. He was very professional and efficient. After he determined nothing was wrong with me, he cleared me for boot camp. I lost Huy for a little bit while going through the many different stations, but we met up again at the end of the day to have the official swearing-in ceremony.

We all filed into the conference room and were told by the sergeant to remain standing at the position of attention. A few seconds later, the sergeant called the room to attention as a captain entered. He congratulated us on passing the rigorous MEPS screening. The time had come for all of us to be true patriots of this great nation by serving in his military. His short speech was very eloquent and patriotic. It gave me goose bumps. We all proudly raised our right hands while facing our nation's flag and pledged our allegiances to the United States. We swore to defend the constitution of the United States and our country against all enemies, foreign or domestic and also to serve the best that we can. I felt very patriotic during the swearing-in ceremony. This was the first time in my life I officially swore to defend the country in a military capacity. I repeated every sentence with pride and gratitude. I was really proud of all of us in that room. I was especially proud of Huy and myself for enlisting.

We left Oakland that evening and returned to San Mateo. It was a very long day, but Huy and I both felt it was well worth it. We shook hands with our recruiter and told him we would see him again the following week when he would take us to the airport.

That night when I arrived home, it finally hit me that I was leaving my baby for at least six months. A feeling of sadness hit me as I sat there watching Briana play with her toys on our bed. Six months is a long time, I thought to myself, but I have to do it. I have to do it for myself, my family, and our family's future. With that in mind, I regained my focus and the sense of direction.

Basic Training at Ft. Sill, Oklahoma

THEN THE DAY came, August 17, 1993. The day I was scheduled to fly to Fort Sill, Oklahoma. I hugged and kissed Briana and Joy for one last time before I left the house. I stopped by my mother's house on South Freemont Street in San Mateo and said good bye to her. She wished me well and told me to be strong. She asked me to call her when I could to let her know I was safe and doing well. I told her I loved her with all my heart and that I would return home soon. As I departed her house, she gave me one last gentle smile as to say, "I love you, my son. Go make me proud."

That morning, Huy and I met our recruiter at the armory at 0500 hours. He drove us to the San Francisco International Airport for the seven-o'clock flight. I had a medium-sized luggage with me. Huy and I were told by our recruiter not to bring too many personal items because right after we get there, the drill sergeants will take them and store them away until we finished with training. Our recruiter advised us that the Army will provide us with "everything" once we hit the ground at Fort Sill. Now looking back, we realized that our recruiter wasn't lying to us when he said that.

We arrived at SFO early that morning around 0620 hours. It was real early in the morning. That was one thing that I was starting to notice about the military—everything was done real early in the morning. I did not understand why, but I would learn really quick why that was the case.

We flew out of SFO at approximately 0800 hours headed for Kansas. We were supposed to catch a connecting flight from Kansas to our final destination. The first leg of our trip was very uneventful, just like how I like it to be. We arrived in Kansas about three hours later and were told we had to wait three hours for our connecting flight. By the time we got on the next plane, it was nearly 1600 hours because of the time zone difference of two hours. Our flight to Oklahoman took only one hour. We arrived and met the Fort Sill reception party at the airport. They welcomed us to Oklahoma and told us we were waiting for more soldiers to fly in before taking us to our base. As we sat there and waited, we saw more and more new young faces get off the plane and they were greeted with the same greetings from the reception folks. By the time everyone arrived, it was getting dark. We piled into a Greyhound bus, and the driver began driving. With the driver was an old sergeant who was there to ensure accountability. He told us we would be transported to the reception area where we would stay for the next few days while we completed the final paperwork.

At first, I was thinking that basic training wasn't going to be as bad as how some of my friends back home had warned me it would be. The sergeant seemed pretty nice. He didn't yell at us once during that bus ride. But I still told myself to be prepared for the worse once we arrived at Fort Sill. I was thinking how mean could the drill sergeants be? Would I make it through this boot camp? What if I couldn't make it through the program? There were so many other things that were racing through my head. Since Huy and I enlisted as battle buddies, we stuck together during this bus ride.

After the long bus ride from the airport, we finally arrived at the Fort Sill reception area. The reception week was where my transformation from civilian life to the Army world began. Shortly after our bus came to a halt, I could feel the tension all around me from everyone on that bus. The air was filled with anxiety and fear. The bus door opened up. A drill sergeant walked onto the bus and said out loud, "Get off my bus now. You guys have one minute to dismount." We all hurried as fast as we could. Huy and I sat in the middle of the bus, so we got off in relatively good time. It was the guys that sat in the back of the bus that had to rush a little more than we did. We all got off the bus in only fifty-five seconds. Phew, we dodged the first test. However, they would always find something that someone apparently did wrong. In this case, our formation was wrong. We had too many guys in the back and not enough in the front. The drill sergeant ordered all of us to drop and made us do four sets of twenty push-ups. When we completed that task, we got up and tried to get in the right formation, but this time there were too many people in the front and not enough in the back. He ordered us to drop again and made us do another four sets of twenty push-ups. By now, my chest was really pumped, but sore. We got up again and tried to get the formation right.

I guess the third time was a charm. Our formation looked just right. He said we were off the hook for at least one hundred flutter kicks. I didn't know what flutter kicks were, but I was just glad I did not have to learn it that night. I learned later what they were from other recruits there. The drill sergeant called out our names and assigned us building numbers so that we could go and rack out for the night. He told us to wake up at 0430 hours and not to be late to his formation at 0445 hours. We quickly got in line and received our bedsheets and pillows before bedding down. Huy and I were assigned to the same building for the reception period.

The next morning we all got up on time, and no one was late to the formation. We marched to the dining facility, also known as the DFAC, for breakfast. We were given two minutes to chow down our meals. I don't think I chewed any of my food that morning. I pretty much swallowed the bread, egg and sausage all at once. After breakfast, we spent the rest of the morning and part of the afternoon getting issued our Physical Fitness Uniforms (PTs), Battle Dress Uniforms (BDUs), boots, field jackets, TA-50 [Kevlar, vest, etc.], and other miscellaneous items from the supply facility [CIF]. Even the civilians that were working at the CIF were bossing us around. We were not getting any love from anyone at all. The afternoon was spent at the barbershop getting all our hair shaved off.

We marched everywhere we went. If you even breathe wrong, you were doing some sort of push-up, sit-up, or jumping jacks. I did my share of push-ups and sit-ups the first day. We also learned how to make our bunks with hospital corners. We were given advice from other recruits who arrived there a few days before us to start practice sleeping on top of our covers in order to save time. They told us once we got to our real training area, we would not have enough time in the morning to make our beds like the way the drill sergeants want you to. So, our group began sleeping on top of our covers the rest of our time at the reception battalion.

The next few days we went through an innumerable amount of shots, attended many orientation briefings, received our ID cards, signed every document you could think of, conducted barracks maintenance, practice Drill and Ceremony, and of course organized Physical Training (PT.) It wasn't until toward the end of our reception week that the drill sergeant started to tell us about how it was a different world "across the tracks." He told us that was where our basic training would start.

"Across the tracks" was both literal and figurative in its meaning. While at the reception area, other recruits would talk about being "across the tracks." They made it sound like it was a hell hole, a place where drill sergeants swarm like crocodiles. I just assumed it meant a training area where we would be for the next ten weeks. Every other day, we saw new recruits being loaded into cattle cars headed for "across the tracks."

Then our day came when we had to get into these cattle cars and head for "across the tracks." I was a little nervous that morning. I was worrying about what was going to happen once we arrived "across the tracks." I got really nervous as we were standing there in formation with my two newly issued duffle bags and a personal bag waiting for the cattle car to arrive. It was very warm that late August morning. There was no cool breeze anywhere. I was sweating profusely while gripping my bags tightly.

There must have been 150 of us in our formation that morning. We were broken up into three groups of fifty. Huy was in my group, which was the first of the three. He was standing just to my right. I looked at him and he, too, was sweating like a pig. I looked around at the people in my group, and I noticed some dude had two Louis Vuitton suit cases. I was thinking, come on dude, are you kidding me? You brought Louis Vuitton suit cases to basic training? Well, at least I knew he would be the one person the drill sergeants would focus their attention on initially instead of me or Huy.

Then three cattle cars arrived in front of our formation. Two drill sergeants emerged from each cattle car. Their uniforms were nicely pressed and their boots were shiny. They had their Smokey the Bear drill sergeant hats on. The two drill sergeants from the middle car came up to our group and asked us how we were doing and if we were treated well during the past week while at the reception area. I knew right away this was a trick. They were way too nice. Just like my mother used to tell me, "If it's too good to be true, then it is." I quickly looked at their name tapes on their uniform and noticed the shorter guy who reminded me of the Tasmanian Devil was Drill Sergeant Ewing and the taller one was Drill Sergeant Welch. They were both Caucasians. After exchanging a few pleasantries, the drill sergeants asked us to load up in the middle cattle car. And when I say cattle car, I mean it was literally a real cattle car. They packed us in there like a can of sardines. We started driving toward the "tracks."

It was the beginning of a very surreal experience. The drill sergeants were also with us inside the cattle car. They did not say a word until we crossed over the railroad tracks. Then all of a sudden, it seemed like a switch was turned on. Drill Sergeant Ewing screamed out from the top of his lungs and ordered us to put our heads down. I knew our military training had just begun. He then ordered us to shut our mouths, close our eyes and listen up. I could still remember his words verbatim to this day. He said, "You are now entering my training area. This area belongs to the drill sergeants, and we own you. You will not be able to do anything without our permission. We will tell you when you can breathe, eat, sleep, shit, shave and shower. For the next ten weeks, you are all ours. Is that understood?" That was really intimidating. We responded with a thunderous reply of, "Yes, drill sergeant."

Drill Sergeant Welch then started yelling at us to pick up our junk off the floor of their cattle cars and hold onto them until we arrived at our training area. I slung one of the duffle bags on my back while holding the other with my right hand. I had my personal bag in my left hand. It was as if they had rehearsed yelling at new recruits the night before or something because as soon as one drill sergeant was done yelling, the other would begin. Drill Sergeant Ewing told us to keep our eyes shut until he told us we could open them. While I was standing there following his instructions and minding my own business, I could feel him come up and stand to the side of my face and check on me. I could feel his warm breath. I guess he wanted to make sure I was not peeking or anything.

A few minutes later, we arrived at our training area. The screaming began again, but this time both drill sergeants were screaming at the same time ordering us to get off their cattle cars. As we were piling off, some people dropped their bags on the way out, so they had to bend down and pick them up. Others fell from being pushed behind. My heart was beating fast and heavy as I was trying to get to the door myself. Outside the door, there were more drill sergeants waiting for us. It was a scene of total chaos. It was like we were being thrown into a pond of starving crocodiles. I finally got off the cattle car and did not know where to go. I looked around and saw at least twenty drill sergeants running around screaming at people from our groups. Some of us were barely out of high school and many had never been yelled at in their entire lives. I find it funny now, but I was pretty terrified then.

I saw that some of us were getting into a formation, so I followed. Not soon after I got in formation, Drill Sergeant Ewing appeared right in front of me. His nose was almost touching mine. I was thinking to myself, "Oh Lord. This was not going to be pretty." Sure enough, he started screaming at me because I had forgotten to take the duffle bag off my back. He asked me why I was in the formation with a duffle bag on. I didn't know what to say, so I looked directly at him. I learned new things the hard way and one thing was: you don't look at a drill sergeant directly in his or her eyes. This was known as "eyeballing." Drill Sergeant Ewing followed up by asking me, "Are you eyeballing me, boy? What? You don't like me? You want to beat me up?"

I was thinking to myself I was going to get smoked for this. Sure enough, he dropped me and made me do push-ups until he came back. The guy that was standing next to me also got Drill Sergeant Ewing's wrath. Soon, he was doing push-ups together with me. It seemed like we both were doing push-ups forever before Drill Sergeant Ewing told us to stop and get back in formation. I was exhausted at this point, but I knew it would not be over just yet. This chaotic scene went on for more than an hour in the assembly area. I thought it would never end. I ended up doing more push-ups and sit-ups by the time they had us all in formations.

We were broken down into three platoons. I was assigned to 1st Platoon, Bravo Battery, 1st Battalion of 19th Field Artillery. I looked for Huy and realized he was in the 2nd Platoon instead of being with me.

We were all drenched in sweat. A tall, huge African American drill sergeant got in front of the formation and told us all to shut up and listen to what he had to say. The entire place got quiet really fast. He introduced himself as the First Sergeant for the battalion and that we were in his training facility. He told us that for the next ten weeks, he and his drill sergeants owned us and they would turn us into lean and mean fighting machines. The ten weeks could be really good or they could be really bad, depending how much of an effort we wanted to put in. He went on to talk about other things before officially introducing the drill sergeants to each platoon.

For my platoon, we would get Drill Sergeants Castilleja, Ewing, and Welch. I thought, "Great. Drill Sergeant Ewing already had my number. For the next nine weeks, I'm toast."

After the First Sergeant was done with his speech, he turned the formation back over to the drill sergeants. The chaos started again. Our barracks were on the third floor of this star shaped building. Drill Sergeant Ewing started screaming we had five minutes to get ourselves, and all of our bags up into the bay or else we were toast. There was no orderly way of completing this process at all. Not in the amount of time we had been given. It was every man for himself. There was only one stairwell up to the third floor. We were prohibited to use the elevator. We all pushed and clawed our way into the stairwell. The stairwell was now full of recruits and their bags. We weren't the only platoon that was trying to get to our bay. The 2nd and 3rd platoon recruits were also trying to get to their bays too. We did not even come close to the allotted five minutes. We finally got into our bay. Drill Sergeant Welch told us to go stand at our bunk in alphabetical order.

Then the fun really began. Drill Sergeant Castilleja said we all really stunk and we needed to go take a quick shower. They told us we had one minute to get out of our BDU's and get into the shower. I have never gotten undressed so

BRIAN HUYNH TRAVIS

fast in my life, but I made it happen. We all grabbed our brown issued towels and ran toward the showers. They told us we had two minutes to get in there, shower, and come back out. I was thinking to myself again, "Two minutes. Are you kidding me?" There was no way we could get fifty guys through the showers in two minutes. Unless there were fifty showerheads in there, it was impossible.

Sure enough, as soon as we got into the shower area, I noticed there were only eight showerheads. So we all piled into these eight shower stalls and just tried to get some water on our bodies. I was rubbing up against guys I had just met. I thought this was crazy, but as long as no one grabbed me the wrong way, then we were all good. We did not all get back out to the bay in time, so they told us to drop and start doing push ups. The only thing we had covering us was the brown towels. So we all got down and started doing push-ups. After about twenty push-ups, they told us to get up and start doing jumping jacks. I was thinking to myself again, "What you talking about, Willis? Do jumping jacks?" A lot of us had this confused look on our faces and were slow to start. Drill Sergeant Welch yelled out, "Drill Sergeant Castilleja, I don't think they heard you."

That was enough to get us all going on the jumping jacks. For most of us, our brown towels fell off our bodies on the first or second jumping jack. I stopped and was going to bend down to pick my towel up, but Drill Sergeant Ewing put a stop to that real quick. He got in my face and told me, "Don't you dare touch that towel! Keep doing your jumping jacks, boy!." Now there were fifty new recruits doing jumping jacks buck naked. The scene was very comical. I could tell the drill sergeants were having a blast as they were laughing underneath their Smokey the Bear hats. I had a recruit in front of me, so the entire time I was looking up at the ceiling while doing these jumping jacks. I noticed he was looking up at the ceiling too. After about two sets of twenty-five jumping jacks, we were again given two minutes to get in the shower.

This time we wised up. We all got in there and turned the water on as if we were showering, but none of us actually showered. We knew they were trying to get us to start thinking like a team. We all decided we would wait a few seconds and then return to our bunks way before the two minutes were up. We returned and stood at the front of our bunks waiting to see what other forms of punishment we were about to endure.

They told us to dig into our duffle bag and get out a new set of BDU's and put it on. By now, it was lunchtime, so they told us we had five minutes to get back in formation in our assembly area. So we all ran toward the stairwell and made our way down to the assembly area. Nothing was orderly on the first day, except when we marched to lunch and dinner. Other than that, everything else was done through chaotic environments. That was how the drill sergeants liked it.

We got to the dining facility and Drill Sergeant Ewing gave us orders not to speak to each other. He said it was not a time to socialize. We were there to eat and drink water to survive, not to enjoy. We were not allowed to have any type of burgers, pizzas, hot dogs, fried chicken, french fries, onion rings, soda, ice cream, or cake. However, we were allowed to eat vegetables, fruits, and other healthy foods and could only drink water and juices.

Once inside the dining facility, it was like a production line. I got my tray, moved to the food line, got my healthy food, moved to the drink line, and got a cup of water. I went to the table, sat down, and shoveled all my food down within thirty seconds. I got up, walked over to where we place our dirty trays, and put mine down. I directly walked outside and got back in formation. This whole process probably took less than five minutes. Now that was efficient.

We marched back to our barracks and continued on with getting smoked the rest of the afternoon. Getting "smoked" meant that we were getting hammered with push-ups, sit-ups, flutter kicks, scissor kicks, and jumping jacks. They found anything and everything that we did wrong and smoked us for our errors. In between being scrutinized for all our actions, we completed some additional paperwork and finished inventory of all our bags. The drill sergeant went through everyone's bags and inspected everything in them. What they were looking for was contraband; i.e., candy, cigarettes, personal weapons, soft drinks, Twinkies, etc.

When it came to my turn to dump everything from my personal bag onto the bed, I got really nervous. I had forgotten that my wife had bought me a bunch of gummy bears and other sweet goodies. As I was dumping everything out, the drill sergeants were in awe of all the gummy bear bags that were falling out. Drill Sergeant Ewing asked me if I intended on opening up a candy shop in his bay. If I was, he would like to get in on my business. My answer was, "No, drill sergeant." They promptly confiscated all my gummy bears and other goodies and moved onto the next poor recruit. They did not let me get off that easy. I was given orders to start pushing and if I could no longer push to turn over and do sit-ups. Once again, I got smoked.

We got a reprieve from the smoking sessions because of dinner that evening. I was starving because I had expended all of my energy during these smoking sessions. We came back from dinner and got smoked the rest of the night. I thought it would never end.

BRIAN HUYNH TRAVIS

We were finally allowed to go to bed that night around 2330 hours. We were all very exhausted. Before we could lie down, the drill sergeants came up with a list of "Fire Guards" for our bay. The drill sergeants explained that the "Fire Guard" would work in two-hour shifts and this person would walk around our bay, making sure no one was going to do anything illegal and watch out for potential fires. The list was in alphabetical order from people's first letter of their last names. I was so happy to hear that because the first letter of my last name started with an which meant I would not have to do watch for a couple of days. Before the drill sergeants left for the night, they told us to wake up at 0430 hours and to be in their formation at 0445 hours.

After they left, I didn't even have the energy to go brush my teeth that night. I changed into my PT uniform and crashed out on my bunk. I felt really bad for the guys that had to do "Fire Guard" that night.

In a blink of an eye, it was 0430 hours. The "Fire Guard" that was supposed to turn on our lights at 0430 hours apparently fell asleep. It was a really bad morning for our platoon. Our drill sergeants arrived and saw that our lights were still off and then saw the "Fire Guard" was snoring. Man, did they go off on us. They flipped the light switch on and began flipping our bunks. My bunk was close to the stairwell door, so I woke up on the cold floor of the bay after Drill Sergeant Ewing flipped my bunk. All I could hear him yell from the top of his lungs was, "Get on your feet now! Now . . . now . . . now. You'd better be down in my formation in two minutes!" Just imagine waking up to your bunk being flipped and having this Tasmanian Devil yelling in your face, "Get on your feet now . . . now . . . now." I think that would give one nightmares for years to come. Later in life, I really appreciated everything the drill sergeants did to us during basic training.

That morning we were smoked from approximately 0405 hours until breakfast time at 0630 hours. They gave us a fifteen minute window to shower, brush our teeth, shave, and get into our BDU's. We marched to breakfast, ate as fast as we could, and we marched back to our assembly area.

While we were in formation waiting for the auditorium to open up to attend some ethics class, I had another direct contact with Drill Sergeant Ewing. He asked me how to pronounce my name because he had not come across a name like mine before. I told him it was pronounced like, "Hew-in." So he asked me if I said "Like, Hew-in? Instead of replying, "Yes, Drill Sergeant" I made a stupid mistake of saying, "Yea, Drill Sergeant." I didn't realize what I had just said until he repeated what I had said. By the time I realized my mistake, it was too late. He was already running with this one. He turned to Drill

Sergeant Welch and said, "Hey, we have a new friend. I asked Private Huynh something and he said, 'yea,' Drill Sergeant." Drill Sergeant Welch egged it on. He asked me what my first name was. I knew I was done. Other recruits were trying to inch away from me as they knew what was about to happen. I told Drill Sergeant Welch my first name was Brian. Drill Sergeant Ewing had this devious smile on his face and walked up to my face and said, "Hey, Brian, let's just call each other by our first names, okay? Is that all right with you?" I nervously replied with, "No, Drill Sergeant." For some reason, I must not have said it loud enough, because he asked me to say it again. It seemed all the drill sergeants were hard of hearing, so you must shout your response at the top of your lungs every time. I followed up with an apology and promised I would never make the same mistake again.

Drill Sergeant Ewing got in my face again and said, "You damnright you will never make that same mistake again, Private. Now get down and start doing the flutter kicks until I tell you to stop." I screamed out, "Yes, Drill Sergeant" from the top of my lungs and promptly went into the flutter kick position. Apparently, I was not doing it right, because he ordered me to stop and chastised me on how his grandmother could do a better flutter kick than I could. He told our platoon to gather around me and that I would be his demonstrator. He wanted to ensure that we all knew the proper way of performing a flutter kick. He explained that flutter kicks are a four-count exercise and the proper way of performing the flutter kick was to lie flat on my back with feet and head approximately six inches off the ground. He told me to place my hands under my buttocks to ensure my fists were clenched to support my lower back. On count one, I would raise my left leg to a forty-five-degree angle, keeping the right leg stationary. On count two, I would raise my right leg off the ground to a forty-five-degree angle, and at the same time moving my left leg to the starting position. Counts three and four are repetition of the same movements. My legs must be locked and my toes have to be pointing away from my body. He asked if the platoon understood how to perform a correct flutter kick from now on. Everyone screamed out, "Yes, Drill Sergeant." In the meantime, he told me to keep going. I kept going and going until I hit muscle failure and couldn't do them anymore. He told me to get up and get back in formation since we were about to go inside the auditorium for classes. I was very relieved.

After the initial first few days of hell, the rest of the first week went by pretty fast. We were very busy each day. We went through a slew of mandatory classes, such as sexual harassment, ethics, and many others. We had the Army values memorized by the end of our second day. The drill sergeants often stopped us out of the blue and asked us to recite them. If we did not remember them, we would be pushing for a while, so all of us made sure we memorized them. I can still recite the values without even thinking about them: loyalty, duty, respect, selfless service, honor, integrity, and personal courage. We were also given the initial physical training(PT) test. I was pretty athletic back then. I did approximately one hundred push-ups, seventy or so sit-ups and ran the two-mile run in under thirteen minutes. My score was somewhere in the high 290's. My score was the second or third best in my platoon. That somewhat impressed my drill sergeants.

By the time we were done with our first two weeks, we had learned to do what we were told, when we were told, and exactly how we were told. We learned quickly that the word "why" no longer existed in our vocabulary, and that they had total control of all of us. We also learned our drill sergeants absolutely loved to make us do push-ups. Their favorite phrase was, "Drop and give me twenty!" One could get dropped for push-ups individually, or with another trainee, or with the entire platoon. We were busy all day and every day. Sundays were the only time we get a few hours off to attend church services. If you did not go to church, you worked on area beautification crews or at the dining facility on kitchen police (KP) duties. We definitely learned not to "eye ball" a drill sergeant when speaking to them, or call them "Sir," because not only would you get smoked, but you would also receive this long lecture about how they work hard for a living. Among many other things we learned during our first two weeks was to always secure your wall locker. We all learned the hard way to never try to outsmart our drill sergeants.

One of the requirements of basic training was to keep your locker locked at all times. Because spinning a combination lock can use up valuable time, especially in the morning, there was a trick that we all tried in the beginning. Locking the lock, but then spinning the right combination, so it is really unlocked and could be opened by a mere pull. However, the drill sergeants caught onto this trick, and they made an example out of the few lockers they found that had the locks in this position.

I still can remember that one day when the drill sergeants went through our bay and found these few lockers with these locks. We were down in our assembly area getting ready to start on another task when one of the drill sergeants came down and started screaming for us to come back up to our bay. Immediately, we knew we were in trouble. By the time we got there, our entire bay floor was strewn with items that they had taken from these lockers. They screamed at us for about five minutes and then proceeded with smoking the entire platoon for a few folks' mistakes.

Let me just tell you that it wasn't very pretty by the time they got through with us. You see, they rarely punished just the violator or violators. They usually punished the entire platoon if one of us messed up or all of us messed up. It did not matter to them. They were trying to teach us that in battle if one person messed up, the entire platoon could die. It was a very good lesson to learn. After this incident, no one would dare to take any more shortcuts with their locks.

So, a typical day for us in Basic Training was:

0430 hours—Wake up
0445 hours—Physical Training
0630 hours—Breakfast
0800 hours—Training
1200-1300 hours—Lunch
1300 hours—Training
1700 hours—Dinner
1800 hours—Drill Sergeant Time
2030 hours—Personal Time
2130 hours—Lights Out

During our third week, our drill sergeants appointed our platoon trainee chain of command. Right before they told us who would be picked for certain leadership position, they called me in their office and asked me how old I was and what I did back home. I told them I was twenty-three years old but already had a lot of life experience under my belt. Twenty-three years old by no means was old to me, but when over 90 percent of your fellow trainees were between the ages of eighteen to twenty, you were considered old and matured. After they asked me those few questions, they promptly kicked me out of their office. A few minutes later, they called our platoon to attention and announced the trainee chain of command. To my surprise, I was chosen as the Platoon Guide (PG) for my platoon. The top dawg, so to speak. I had an Assistant Platoon Guide (APG) under me and also four squad leaders.

They gave us each a red armband with yellow sergeant stripes with a star in the middle. We each looked at our new armbands with admiration and pride. We safety pinned them onto our left upper arms and just stared at them for a quick moment, as if we were all on cloud nine. Then we fell out of the sky and got back to reality when the drill sergeants came out of their office and told us not to get comfortable with our positions, because we could be fired at anytime. We all told them we would do our best and also try not to let our fellow trainees down. After the appointment, I called a meeting with my APG and the four squad leaders. We went over plans on how to intervene and solve issues of soldiers within our platoon. After a short meeting, we came up with plans on how to deal with pretty much everything. Some of these plans were: which squad would be in charge of buffing the bay for that week, cleaning the latrines, performing "Fire Guards" at night, conducting police calls around our platoon assembly area, and so on. I also broke down each squad even further by having three teams with three members in each. Each team would have a team leader. And the team leaders would report to their squad leaders. This way it would afford members within my platoon to gain some leadership experience and prepare them to take over if our current chain should be fired for any reason at all.

I told my squad leaders I wanted to implement our plans immediately. They agreed. I then requested and received permission from our drill sergeants to call a meeting with the entire platoon so that I could speak to them about how we could help each other for the rest of our time at Ft. Sill, and that our leadership chain would be there to help them solve any issues they might face. I asked them to bring these issues up through their chain of command within their squads instead of going straight to the drill sergeants. As I was addressing the platoon, I could tell some members in the crowd were not very happy that I was selected. I didn't really know why at the time, but a couple of my squad leaders came up to me later that night and told me there were a few folks that did not think I should lead because I was Asian.

Learning about this initially made me upset, but the more I thought about it, the more I told myself to let things play themselves out. Some of the things I realized or assumed were a few of these trainees probably came from areas where there were no minorities, especially Asians, and that might be the reason(s) why they were objecting to having an Asian leading the platoon. They probably thought, because I was Asian, I would be passive and weak while leading the platoon. If that was the reason, then they had no idea who I was and where I came from, because I was the exact opposite. If anything, I would be too aggressive and speak my mind when I should be listening.

My bunkmate to the right of me was another Vietnamese. What a surprise. What were the chances of that? He was subsequently assigned as my battle buddy because he was next to me. He was a good guy. We went everywhere together. He was like my Siamese twin. He was a little bit older than I was. Everything he did wrong I got smoked for with him. Everything I did wrong he got smoked with me. We became pretty good friends as the training went on. He was eventually chosen by our drill sergeants to be our permanent guidon bearer. As for Huy, he stayed in 2nd Platoon for the duration. We still got to see each other during training and other activities, so it was not all that bad.

A couple of days after my appointment, I had my first challenge. One night, two of the squad leaders came up to me and my APG and reported their guys were giving them a hard time for making them work too hard. You see, we had to buff our bay and clean the latrines every night and every morning, so we had assigned different squads to switch off cleaning assignments on a weekly basis. This one night, one squad was assigned to buff the bay while another squad was assigned to clean the latrines. The squad leaders told me their guys felt like the floors and the latrines were shiny and clean enough to pass the drill sergeants' inspection in the morning. Knowing our drill sergeants and their high expectations of how a shiny floor should look like, my APG and I conducted our own pre-inspection check.

As soon as we walked into the bay, we could see that floors were not shiny at all. That got me a little upset. We walked into the latrine and noticed it was still dirty. I saw the sinks were not wiped off completely. I went out and called a platoon meeting. I told them I was not happy with the efforts these two squads had put in with their cleaning assignments and I wanted to see more out of them. Then I had a couple of smart alecks in the background saying if we wanted the floor to be shinier, why didn't we go ahead and buff the floors ourselves? That really infuriated me, because my APG and I did join different squads each week to help them clean our bay. We were not the type of leaders that just sit back and watch everyone else clean because of our positions. I made sure my squad leaders also clean with their squads each time. So for those guys to say that—it made me, my APG, and my squad leaders really upset.

Soon, more folks joined in and told us we hadn't been doing anything to help and that all we did was ordering them around. Again, this was not true. For some reason, I just lost it. I started screaming every bad word in my vocabulary out loud and challenged to fight me. I told them I would take on every single one of them either one on one or one on forty-four. I called every single one of them out. Next thing I knew my APG and my squad leaders joined in. We kept calling the rest of the platoon out. We told them that if they wanted changes, then they would have to beat us up, but if not they were to shut up and go along with the program. None of them stepped forward to accept our challenge. After a few minutes, I told the platoon that our meeting was over and the two squads that were responsible for buffing the floor and cleaning the latrines to finish what they were doing or I would get more upset. They grudgingly went back and finished their duties the right way. After they were done, my APG and I did our second pre-inspection and this time everything was clean in the latrine, and the floor was shiny.

The next morning, the drill sergeants arrived and right away they called me into their office. Apparently, they knew about the incident from the night before, so they asked me what happened. I told them everything. After they were satisfied that I did not lie, they told me to get out of their office. However, on my way out, I heard Drill Sergeant Ewing say out loud, "You are a crazy, Private." I didn't think anything of it and kept walking. Thinking back now, I think that was one of the incidents where I had gained some respect from my platoon. Soon after, I did not have any issues with anyone in my platoon. They did not question anything my APG, their squad leaders or I asked them to do. Actually, people started coming up to me for advice and for mentorship. One piece of advice that I didn't give to anyone was to "lie low." That was not a realistic piece of advice. The drill sergeants looked for folks who did try to lie low, and they would make it a point to get them out of their comfort zone. I would tell them to be themselves, be motivated and helpful in everything that they do. For those that the drill sergeants thought were trying to lie low, they started assigning "pseudo" leaders. Our chain of command was fired on many different occasions between the third and fourth weeks. People that tried to lie low were placed in our positions for as short as a few hours or for as long as the entire day.

The rest of our third week went by really fast, and before we knew it, we were introduced to our rifles on our fourth week. We did not get to shoot them until week five. The drill sergeants made sure we knew that our rifles were not called "guns." They were "M16A2 rifles." If you were ever heard calling your rifle a "gun," then you would be doing push-ups for a while. We were pretty excited to get our hands on these rifles. For the next few days, we learned how to hold it, march with it, point it, take it apart, clean it, put it back together, take it apart again, put it together again, take it apart once more, put it back together again, and always have it within our sight. Pretty soon, most of us could completely disassemble and reassemble our rifles with our eyes closed.

On our fifth week, the drill sergeants told us the original trainee chain of command would be permanent. I felt relieved that we now could just concentrate on the very crucial next few weeks before winding down our training. Being in a leadership position was very challenging while you were going through the same training like everyone else. It required a lot of extra time and stress. It required we sacrifice a lot of our free time in order to get everything to run just right. It was also a lot of responsibilities, but without all the perks and no "real" authority. However, it was excellent leadership training for those of us that were fortunate to have been given the opportunity to lead. We were introduced to the Basic Rifle Marksmanship during this week. This was where we learned how to shoot with our beloved M16A2 rifle. We learned a lot more than just pulling the trigger. We learned how to properly hold our rifles, the breathing pattern prior to pulling the trigger, and how to shoot from many different positions. Everything we learned in week four was very helpful during this week. It just all tied in.

Our drill sergeants told us that there was a competition between our three platoons within Bravo Battery to see which platoon would have the most "expert shooters." We learned that in order to become shoot experts, we had to hit thirty-five out of forty targets on qualification day. Our prize, if our platoon won this competition, would be an extended personal time on the evening of the qualification day. We were all pumped up, because we really needed the extra time to get our personal things in order, like writing an extra letter home to our families, getting some extra sleep, doing an extra load of laundry, or just relaxing for a minute. The next few days, our platoon really came together as a team. We all helped each other out with just about everything and anything. The camaraderie among everyone was at an all-time high.

The qualification day came. We got on the bus that morning and went to the range to qualify. We arrived and got ready for this big competition. Safety on the range was paramount, so the drill sergeants were really on edge. This was not the day for you to screw up. Luckily, no one did, and there were no accidents of any sort. Everyone in our platoon tried really hard to do well, but at the end of that day, we only had seven or so expert shooters while 3rd platoon had way more than we did. I was one of the seven shoot experts. I hit thirty-nine out of forty targets. We had not one in our platoon that hit forty out of forty targets that day. The best part was everyone in our platoon qualified on their first try. In order to qualify, we had to hit at least twenty-three out of forty targets. For that I was happy. At least we got a little bit of a break while we waited to take part in the night fire. The drill sergeants made sure it was pitch-black before they allowed us to start shooting. We conducted night fire without any night vision equipment on our rifles. We had tracer rounds that helped a lot. We were out on the range until very late. That next morning, we were allowed to sleep an extra hour.

Those of us who were qualified experts on the range received our expert badges. We had a battery formation. When it came to our platoon, our drill

BRIAN HUYNH TRAVIS

sergeants called the seven qualified experts to the front of the formation. We were all really proud of ourselves. The drill sergeants asked us if we wanted them to hand us the badges or if we would like to receive them by the way of "blood badges." We all said, "Blood badges, Drill Sergeants." We all didn't really know what "blood badges" really meant, but it sounded like some mystical ritual or military custom that has been around for centuries and to be a part of it would be really unique.

Then the drill sergeants had our entire platoon in single file line and began walking toward the seven of us. The drill sergeants explained that each member of our platoon would walk by and congratulate us by tapping the badge that was on the left side of our chest. I quickly looked at my expert badge and realized it had two one-quarter inch prongs on them. I initially held the badge on my left chest, but after the first couple of my platoon mates pounded it into my skin and flesh, I dropped my hand and stood there as the rest of my platoon walked by and congratulated me. It didn't hurt as bad as I thought it would. By the time the fifth or sixth person got to my chest it no longer hurt, because it already had gone numb. It hurt afterward, but I got over the pain real quick. Our drill sergeants did not take part in the ceremony. They never told us the reasons why they did not take part in it, but I am certain it was for some liability issues.

Then next up in our training was the gas chamber. Our drill sergeants told us the day before the gas chamber that we needed to ensure our gas masks were working properly. We did not want to enter the gas chamber with a faulty gas mask. They said it would be a really bad deal unless we loved to suck in ortho-chlorbenzylidenedimalonitrile. This long word is just another word for the active substance in CS tear gas. So that afternoon, we spent time on adjusting our masks to ensure we all had a tight seal and that none of them were defective. On the day of the gas chamber, we were told not to eat too much at lunch, because the food might not stay down. We were instructed once inside the chamber we were to unseal our masks, state our names, our social security number, and our platoon motto, which was "Battle Dragons." Only after you have completed saying what you were supposed to, then you could exit out the back door.

Then the day arrived for the gas chamber. Our Bravo Battery marched out to the gas chamber that morning. When we arrived on scene we stayed in battery formation. All of a sudden, we heard a loud whistle and shortly after, three big explosions. Trainees began calling out, "Gas. Gas. Gas." We knew exactly what to do. We quickly removed our gas masks from our holders and dawned them on our faces. The rest of the morning, we received more training on chemical agents and also the last-minute info on the gas chamber. For lunch we were given Meals Ready-to-Eat (MREs.) This was the first time most of us had seen MREs. It was a self-contained, individual field ration in a lightweight black plastic packaging. I looked at my MRE package and noticed I got spaghetti. I was really stoked. I didn't want something like ham and egg or an omelet or something similar to those meals. At this stage in our training, we were still not allowed to eat sweets, so the drill sergeants told us to turn over any sweets we find in our MREs. I was dying for any type of candy and, low and behold, there two tootsie rolls inside my MRE.

I did the right thing and turned those precious tootsie rolls in to the small bucket the drill sergeants had placed in the middle of the formation. Soon, everyone turned in some sort of sweets. That bucket was filled to the brim with goodies. Or at least we thought everyone had turned in their candy, but that was not the case. The drill sergeants went through the bucket and counted every single piece of candy and somehow discovered there were two pieces of candy missing. They ordered us to get back in formation and asked for those two people to step forward. The drill sergeants warned that if these two made them conduct 100 percent search of all personnel, then these two folks could be kicked out for dishonesty if they were discovered.

Thank God, these folks stepped forward and owned up to the violations. We all got smoked anyway for not "taking care" of our buddies. So now we were exhausted and sweating profusely in these suits. They gave us a quick breather and then we had to line up for gas chamber. I asked our drill sergeants to let me and the APG go first so that we could lead by example. They gladly allowed us to be the first ones in line for our platoon. We put our masks on and went inside with six or eight other trainees. As soon as I stepped inside, I could feel the gas hitting my exposed skin on my hands and the back of my neck. I began to experience a very uncomfortable stinging and burning sensation as if someone had just rubbed a jar of Icy Hot on my rash.

We stood there for a few minutes before the drill sergeant told us to break the seal of our masks and completely take them off. We knew exactly what to do. I took off my mask and began saying out loud my name, rank, social security number, but before I could say our platoon motto, I was overcome by the intense ortho-chlorbenzylidenedimal onitrile effect that I began choking and gasping for air. I had snot running from my nose and tears gushing out of my eyes like I had just got done watching Romeo and Juliet. We all quickly ran outside to get some fresh air. The drill sergeants had set up an area where you go right after exiting from the gas chamber. The only issue was that the area was right next to where other soldiers from the battery were lining up to go into the chamber. I quickly realized this right after I exited the chamber. Being a platoon guide, I did not want to show weakness in front of my peers, so I quickly toughened up as if it didn't really bother me. Those were the most painful and challenging minutes of my life.

After the gas chamber, our time during the rest of basic training flew by. We went through a series of obstacle courses. These courses tested how well we worked together as a team. During this phase of our training, we tested our physical endurance by jumping over walls, running across small pieces of wood, scaling a wall, running through chains formed into squares, and the most dangerous: low-crawling under a barbed wire fence while live machine guns were firing rounds over our heads. That part was nerve-racking, but as long as you had 100 percent trust in the drill sergeants, you were okay. We were introduced to other light weapons in the U.S. Army inventory such as machine guns and M203 grenade launchers. We also got training on hand grenades and had to qualify with them. In order to qualify as an expert, we had to throw the hand grenade into a certain designated zone on the course. This course wasn't hard at all. Many of us qualified expert on this course.

We were trained in the art of land navigation next. We learned how to use a compass, read a map, plot points, etc. By now we were down to our last phase of training. We took our final PT test a few days before our big field training exercise (FTX.) It was a three-day exercise where we would be bused to our FTX site, set up camp and conduct training before culminating into a big exercise. On our final day of this FTX, we would have to ruck march back to our barracks in order to complete the FTX and basically graduate from basic training. A ruck march is when you get your pack, load it with all the essential gear you would need to survive and march with it on your back for a long distance. The distance of this ruck march was fifteen kilometers. If you couldn't ruck march back, then you would get recycled and do boot camp all over again. There was no way anyone would want that. Not after all the things we went through. The last thing you wanted was to go back through again.

Everyone in my platoon was able to make it through the FTX and also the fifteen kilometer ruck march. We felt so relieved when we arrived at our barracks after a very tough three-day exercise.

The last week was all planning for the upcoming graduation ceremony. Our drill sergeants had eased up on smoking us and were now treating us as if we were almost actual trained soldiers and not trainees anymore. I called my mom and asked her if she would be able to fly out to my graduation ceremony. She told me she could not afford the plane ticket and hotel costs, so she would not make it. She did tell me she was very proud of me for graduating basic training. I also called my wife, but we were facing the same dilemma with money. We just didn't have enough to afford plane tickets and hotel for Joy and Briana to come out for the graduation ceremony.

The graduation day came where we all graduated. I ended up being awarded the "Distinguished Honor Graduate" for my battery. I was very proud and humbled by the award. There were many others who also worked very hard and also were deserving of the award.

After the graduation ceremony was over, Huy and I went straight to the airport and boarded a plane for Fort Sam Houston, San Antonio, to begin the next phase of our training. Fort Sam Houston was where we were trained for twelve weeks to become combat medics (91B.) This was part of our Advanced Individual Training (AIT.) It was a lot different than basic training. From the physical training perspective, it was a lot easier than our weeks spent at Ft. Sill. We got "smoked" a lot from these drill sergeants. There were times when I thought I was back in basic training because of some stupid things other trainees did. We were given a lot more personal time to study and take care of our other personal maintenance issues Trainees failed during this phase of training in the academic arena. This phase was mostly about academics more than anything else. The first five weeks we spent a lot of time in the classroom learning about the basic human anatomy and the physiology of how certain parts of our body work. We were given tests on these subjects and we had two chances to pass each test. If you failed your retake test, you were either recycled from the class or were dropped from the class and reclassified to do something else for the Army. I definitely did not want to fail any test twice.

We started out with a really big company. By the midway mark of this training, we had lost over twenty trainees due to academic failures. Most of us were smart enough to make it through the classroom portion, so we were rewarded with some privileges. These privileges included going and staying off post for the weekend if you wanted to. We could eat candy and drink sodas again. We were not supposed to drink was alcoholic beverages. The drill sergeants would be in our Monday morning formations with breathalyzers and if you tested positive for alcohol, then life would be really painful for you. I never had that problem, so I wouldn't know what they would do to you. I have heard stories from others and they weren't pretty. I was too focused in my training and thinking about my family to get into trouble.

BRIAN HUYNH TRAVIS

In the second half of our training, we learned how to triage, draw blood, diagnose patients, set up a casualty point, do patient carries, load patients into an Army ambulance, or MEvac, and treat injured personnel on the battlefield. Whenever I got some free time, I would call home, write to my family, work out at the gym, or sleep in. It was in mid-December and I had been away from my family for four months now. I missed them terribly. Briana was going on thirteen months, and I had missed half of her life already and the important milestones she went through like her first steps and her first birthday. I missed my wife and her beautiful smiles. I missed my mom and her home cooking. It was hard being away for that long, but I knew it was the right thing to do for me, my family, and for our country.

Christmas came really fast. Our drill sergeants spoke to us about the Christmas Exodus. They explained that the Army is the only service that completely shuts down its basic training and advanced individual training for ten days during Christmas time so that staff members and trainees could go home and spend time with their families. The only thing was we had to pay for our own round-trip plane tickets and any leave we would take would come out of our accrued leave entitlement. The other option was we could just stay on post and study or just relax.

I really wanted to come home for the holidays. After calling around for airplane tickets and finding out they would cost me an arm and a leg to fly home, I decided it would be best if I spent that Christmas at Fort Sam Houston. That was another lonely Christmas for me. Most of my friends decided to go home, and so there were only a few of us left. We spent most of the time working out at the gym or traveling to the River Walk Mall in downtown San Antonio to enjoy its beauty.

The River Walk Mall was and still is truly the heart of San Antonio. The people were friendly and very polite. The river and walkway was lined with restaurants, shops, apartments, hotels, and parks. There were boat cruises that operate along the river all day and into the night. Their cruises were quite short, lasting only thirty-five to forty minutes but the nice thing about them was you get a commentary about the establishments along the river. The view of the buildings lining the river was very attractive from the water level. I thoroughly enjoyed my every moment spent at the River Walk Mall.

The ten days went by and we were back to learning. It felt like, in the blink of an eye, we were finished with our course and made plans to return home. After graduating AIT, Huy and I flew back to California. Joy, Briana and my mother met me at the San Francisco International Airport. I was overjoyed at seeing them. Though it was only six months, Briana seemed to have grown so much. She was not running around in her walke and mumbling all sorts of things. She was walking by herself and could say quite a few words. I was so happy to finally come home. I really missed my mother's home cooked meals. I loved everything she cooked. It did not matter what it was and I just loved eating it.

After a short break, Huy and I reported for duty to our National Guard Unit, HHC 2/159th Infantry Battalion (Mechanized) in San Jose. Huy and I were brand spanking new Privates, E-1s. We didn't even have any rank on our collars. Everyone else in our section was either an E-4 or above. Since we were the two lowest ranking people in our unit, Huy and I got stuck with all the hard duties. This was something that we had expected since we were privates. The hard duties did not bother us at all. That was just how we were trained and raised, so we just did what we were told. For the next six years we performed our duties one weekend a month and two weeks a year. We rose through the ranks to E-4s or Specialists. We both attained that rank sometime in 1996. That was where Huy stayed since he did not want to go any higher. I was promoted to the rank of Sergeant or E-5 in 1997. That same year, Sacramento County suffered tremendous flooding due to some very big storms that had hit the area. Our unit was activated to go assist victims from this flood. Huy and I were activated, but we mostly stayed at our unit in San Jose to assist with the logistic issues for soldiers that were deployed to the Sacramento area. This activation only lasted approximately one week and soon it was over. We all returned to our families. The unit was not utilized for any other state emergencies during the rest of my time there.

I completed my National Guard service requirement in 1999, but I still wanted to serve in the Army. I joined the 670th Military Police Company in Sunnyvale. I would later attend Officer Candidate School (OCS) and got my commission in 2001. I joined Bravo Company 250th Military Intelligence Battalion (TEB) shortly after as a platoon leader.

Between me changing my military units and received my commission, I also became a police officer for the South San Francisco Police Department.

South San Francisco Police Department

S OUTH SAN FRANCISCO is a city in San Mateo County. It lies in a small valley just north of San Bruno and the San Francisco International Airport, and south of Daly City, Colma, Brisbane, and the San Bruno Mountains, east of Pacifica and the hills of the Coast Range, and west of the waters of San Francisco Bay. Most of the valley faces San Francisco Bay, affording sweeping vistas from higher levels and a definite sense of identification with the Bay. It has a population of approximately sixty thousand based on the census at the time. It is known as "The Industrial City." It even has the moniker on Sign Hill overlooking the east of Bay Shore Freeway U.S. 101. If you drive northbound on U.S. 101, you will see the moniker on Sign Hill clearly as you near Grand Avenue.

In early 1997, I started taking criminal justice classes at the College of San Mateo. My goal was to eventually become a full-time police officer. I really enjoyed the classes and all the things I was learning. I also came across a guy who was at basic training with me back in 1993. His name was Patrick. He was in 2nd Platoon when we were at Fort Sill. What a small world, I thought. We became really good friends after our reserve classes.

I told my mother I was applying with different police agencies to become a reserve officer and eventually make it a full-time job for me. She was not too supportive at first since she came from a country that looked down upon police officers as corrupt, brutal, or unlettered. Being a police officer was considered a negative in Vietnam, and the job was considered for the uneducated people. I explained to her in depth that being a police officer in America was a lot different than being one in Vietnam. Here police departments expect their officers to possess the utmost integrity and other core values that are important to the public's trust. The salary and benefits here are also so much better than those in most other countries. I reassured her that I would definitely discuss with her further, before making any final decisions, and that made her feel a little bit better. She knew that deep down inside, I wanted to become a police officer.

I also told Joy of my intentions to become a reserve police officer initially, and eventually I would like to make it a full-time career. Just like my mother, Joy initially had some reservations of me making it a full-time job since she considered it a very dangerous job and did not want to see me get hurt. I went through the entire process of reassuring her as I did with my mother earlier about how beneficial the job would be for the family. I got to serve the community and in return our family would get great benefits and good pay. So in the end, Joy was also supportive of my quest to become a police officer.

After completing my reserve police officer classes at College of San Mateo, I began applying to different local agencies to become their reserve police officer. A few weeks after I had applied at the South San Francisco Police Department, I received a letter requesting me to meet at the South San Francisco Police Department to take the physical agility test. I was in very good shape, so I was not worried about this test at all. I showed up at the date and time listed on the letter and saw Ed and Patrick there. We were tested on our endurance with a two-mile run, push-ups, and sit-ups. At the end of the test, we all passed with ease. A few weeks after the physical agility test, I received another letter from the South San Francisco Police Department requesting me to meet with one of their background investigators at their department to discuss my application further. I was happy but naturally nervous at the same time. I did not know what this investigator was going to ask me, but I told myself if I just tell the truth, then I would not have anything to worry about.

I arrived at the South San Francisco Police Department (South City) on the date and time listed on the letter and met with Lieutenant Tealdi. He introduced himself as the background investigator for the police department and shook my hand firmly. He was a tall fellow with a friendly smile. He was in his early fifties with salt and pepper colored hair. He led me to the back conference room. He sat across me and began telling me what they expected from their reserve police officers and all the things I had to do to maintain my reserve officer status if I was hired by South City. He asked me if I would be okay with that. I said yes. His first question was why I wanted to become a police officer. My answer was simple. I have always wanted to help people, fight for the underdog, look out for the unfortunate, and assist in enforcing the laws of our land. I also told him that I wanted a job that would be beneficial for me, my family, and the community. He looked at me with admiration and said, "Brian, you are the kind of guy we would like to have here." He then asked me about my background. I told him I was born in Vietnam and came here in 1979. He had this big smile on his face as soon as he heard I was from

Vietnam. He wanted me to know that he was in Vietnam during the conflict in the early 1970's. He was a colonel in the U.S. Army. He said he really liked Vietnam and its people. We spoke about Vietnam for a few more minutes before getting back to the background interview.

He then went through so many thorough questions on my background form. He asked me things that my mom didn't even know about. Things I would never tell anyone else. He asked about pretty much everything and anything as follows: "Have you ever stolen anything in your life? Have you ever used illegal drugs?" He asked how many times I had gotten into fights and so on. Halfway into our interview, I was already exhausted from answering these very intimate and very personal questions. I realized police agencies need to know who they are getting before hiring someone. No agency wants to make the mistake of hiring a nut case, because of liability issues. I caught my breath and continued answering more questions. He was very thorough with his questioning. I could tell he had been doing this for a while. By the time he was done with the interview, he knew pretty much everything about me—when I was born, how many relatives I had, where they lived, where I grew up at, with whom I hung out, and so on.

I was very fortunate to have not done anything that would disqualify me from continuing on with the hiring process. After the interview, he told me it looked pretty good that I would be hired by South City. He showed me around the department and introduced me to a number of people that were on duty at the time. Everyone I met was so nice and professional. I was just really impressed with the people I had met and how clean and professional the office looked. Lieutenant Tealdi showed me their indoor shooting range and their patrol vehicles parked in their underground garage. I was really excited about the possibility of being a part of such a stellar organization. He told me not to get too excited yet, because there were a few more critical tasks I had to complete before I could be hired. One of those remaining critical tasks was the lie detector test. He said this was the test where most people fail because they try to hide things and they get caught. I didn't care at this point what kind of test it was. I just going to tell the truth and let the truth set me free. He wished me luck before escorting me out of the station. That night, I told both Joy and my mother I had a pretty good chance of becoming a reserve officer for South City. They were happy for me.

Then I got a letter from South City to report to an office in Foster City to take my lie detector test. I arrived and met the test administrator. He led me into his office and asked me to sit down next to the lie detector machine. He told me to relax as he needed to place a blood pressure cup on my left arm to monitor my blood pressure, a device on my right index finger to monitor my body temperature and skin conductivity, and some sort of an electrical band around my heart to monitor my heart rate. By the time he was done, I looked like an in patient in an emergency room. He asked me to be honest and answer every question to the best of my ability. I was a little nervous and intimidated with all the things he had placed on my body, but I was ready to get this test over with. I thought he was going to ask me new questions, but that was not the case. He just went over the questions Lieutenant Tealdi had asked me. I guess this process was to make sure I was consistent with my answers on that background form and also to see if I had lied on any of my responses. After about two hours of this arduous process, he was done with me. I didn't think I could take anymore of this guy interrogating me that day. I left his office feeling pretty good about this latest test.

A few more weeks went by without hearing anything from South City. Then I received a letter stating I had passed the background stage and the last tasks were to submit to a psychological test and a medical exam. That was a big sigh of relief knowing I had passed the background test. Though I had nothing to hide, I think the entire background process would make anyone nervous with all the intimate and very personal questions being asked and then it culminates into you wearing all sorts of equipment for the lie detector test.

The next step was the psychological test. I received a letter asking me to respond to the psychiatric doctor in Redwood City for this test. I thought it was no big deal. I was thinking when I got there, the doctor would ask me a few questions, realize I wasn't crazy, and he would finish the test in about five minutes. Boy, I was wrong. I arrived and was asked to sit in the waiting room. There I was asked to complete two booklets of questionnaires. The only problem was these booklets had five hundred questions in each. Five hundred questions in each booklet? What can they possibly want to know? So I opened up the first booklet to see what kind of questions they were asking. I was flabbergasted at the first few questions I saw. They were: "Do you see things that others can't see? Do you talk to the dead? Do you hear voices that others can't hear?" I understood why the doctor needed to know my answers to these questions. He needs to make sure that my mental health was just as good as my physical health.

You just can't have anyone running around trying to serve and protect when they are hearing and seeing things. That person wouldn't be any good for any organization, let alone a police department. So I sat there patiently and completed one thousand questions in the form of two booklets. About two hours later, I was called into the doctor's office. He was old. No, actually he was ancient. He had gray hair and a gray mustache. He asked me to sit down right next to him and began a casual conversation with me. He asked questions that only pertained to the questionnaire I completed from my background investigation. I thought that was weird. I thought he would be asking questions to ensure I was not a nut case, but that was not the case at all. As the session neared its end, I realized that this test was an extension of my background investigation. Besides the two booklets I completed when I first arrived at his office, he didn't really ask me any psychological questions at all.

I left his office a little confused, but again, felt good about my interview with him, so I was very hopeful. A week or two later, I received another letter from South City saying I had passed the psych test. The last and final test was the medical exam. I could almost feel it: being hired as a reserve police officer. I had almost completely stopped hanging out with the boys getting drunk on the weekends. I was really focused on my family and my mother.

I went to the medical exam and discovered it was the most relaxing task of all the tasks in the hiring process. I went to a medical facility listed on their letter and submitted to a full medical exam. It was a piece of cake. They drew some blood, asked me a few questions about my legs and arms, and examined my ears and eyes. Before I knew, it was over.

The last thing I had to do was really for formality purposes and that was to meet with the Police Chief Raffaelli. Lieutenant Tealdi had set up the meeting with Chief Raffaelli beforehand. I arrived and was escorted into the Chief's office by his secretary. This was the first time I had met with any chief of police, so I was very nervous. Chief Raffaelli was a little bit taller than me, but he was broader and you could tell he worked out regularly. He had four stars on his collars, a rank I had seen only in military pictures for a general of the Army. The meeting was really informal. He wanted to congratulate me and welcomed me to his department. He also wanted me to know that I was the first ever Vietnamese officer at South City, and he was hoping one day I would be interested in becoming a full-time police officer. I thanked him for giving me the opportunity to serve the South San Francisco community, and told him I would not let him down. We exchanged a few more conversations about me being in the military and my family's background. Then he pulled out a shiny police reserve badge and handed it to me. He said that it was mine and before I could become an official reserve officer for his department, I had to go with Lieutenant Tealdi down to Human Resources (HR) and get sworn in.

I was so happy. I came out of Chief Raffaelli's office and was immediately greeted by Lieutenant Tealdi and Reserve Captain McCracken. They congratulated me and took me down to HR and had me sworn in. They drove me back to the department and issued me all my gear. They gave me my first duty weapon, a black nine-millimeter Berretta, and two extra magazine clips. I also received my first ever bullet-proof vest. They told me I could not begin working for them until I qualified with my weapon. They walked me over to the range master's office and introduced me to Sgt. Normandy. He congratulated me on being hired as a reserve and asked me to come back in a week for my qualification course. I couldn't wait. I came home that day and showed my family and mother my new reserve badge and all the equipment I had received that day. They were impressed with everything I showed them. My mother told me to be careful when I hit the streets. I reassured her that I could only work with another full-time officer, so I will always be with someone else. That helped ease her fear a little, but mothers will always be mothers. They never stop caring or worrying about you.

I completed qualifying with my duty weapon and other in-house training and before I knew it, I was going on my first work shift. It was swing shift that I wanted to work on that night. Swing shift starts at 1600 hours and end at 0200 hours. I showed up for briefing a little early, so I was hanging out in the hallway where they had all the sworn and reserve officers' pictures in a glass case hung up on the wall. I viewed the pictures of all officers on the wall and noticed a lot of the officers were of Italian descent. Lieutenant Tealdi later explained to me that South City was founded mostly by the Italians and Irish back in the early 1900's. There are a large number of Italians still living in South City, but the majority of the population now consist of Hispanics and Asians. I noticed there were a total of seven minority officers out of eighty. That didn't matter with me. We were all wearing blue, and I was really looking toward being accepted in the brotherhood and sisterhood of the police world.

That night I was assigned to ride with Officer Gil. He was a tall lanky guy. I was sitting in the back of the briefing room. He was sitting near the front of the room. He turned to me and said, "You had better bring your a game tonight if you are riding with me." I wanted to tell him that I bring my game every time I do something but I didn't want him to think I was showing off since it was my first night there. I just told him that I would do my best. After briefing, I followed him to our patrol car. He went over the steps of how to conduct a pre-inspection check of the patrol vehicle before we went into service. After we were done, we were on the streets of South City. It felt weird being in the front seat of the patrol car. I would have never imagined that I would be a police officer when I was growing up and partying all the time. There was a sense of pride, relief, duty, and a new sense of responsibility that hit me all at once.

Officer Gil told me even though South City was considered a mid-sized city in the Bay Area, it did not lack crimes. As he was giving me a quick brief of the city, he noticed a vehicle code violation right in front of him and promptly initiated a traffic stop on the vehicle. I was just in awe how a guy could be in the midst of telling me about a city and then all of a sudden switching to recognizing a violation and pulling the violator over. Everything happened so fast, and he seemed so skilled at what he was doing that it made me really nervous about my capabilities of being able to perform what he just did.

He called the guy's information in and was already done with the citation by the time dispatch came back with the guy's information. Before I knew it, we were done with the traffic stop and got back in the car. Officer Gil never lost a beat. He picked up where he left off and continued to tell me to be ready that night for any possibilities. He said he had a feeling it was going to be a really busy night. I was thinking there was no way it could get busy since it was a weeknight.

Well, I was wrong. We continued to make traffic stops and went to a few loud noise calls. Then the action really started. We were southbound on South Linden Avenue when we heard one of our units and other units from the San Bruno Police Department over the radio. They were in a high-speed pursuit of a vehicle, and the pursuit was heading our way. A few minutes later, there was the suspect's vehicle traveling northbound on South Linden heading straight at us. He looked at me and said, "What did I tell you?" All of a sudden, my heart started racing a hundred miles an hour and my blood pressure shot way up high. I made sure I had my seatbelt on and told myself, "Here we go." As the suspect vehicle raced past us, Officer Gil made a U-turn and pursued the vehicle. We did not see any San Bruno units in the area at all. We heard our lone unit had crashed during the pursuit somewhere in San Bruno. It was just us for now until other units from the west side could join us. Officer Gil started letting dispatch know we were behind the suspect vehicle and we were in pursuit. The perpetrator led us on a pursuit through the streets of South City. We reached speeds of 65-70 mph, sometimes in 25-mph zones. We went through stop signs and red lights. Lucky for us, there was not a lot of foot or vehicle traffic that night in the downtown area. As we neared Eighth Lane, the suspect's vehicle slowed down and it appeared like the driver was going to foot bail. The suspect's vehicle stopped abruptly. A young kid jumped out of the driver seat and began running westbound on Eighth Lane. Officer Gil stopped our patrol car, but he stopped it right next to a parked vehicle. I couldn't get out on my side since I was blocked in. I had to jump over to the driver's seat and get out of the patrol car on that side. To make things worse, as he was getting out, he inadvertently locked his door, so I couldn't open it right away. I had to look around for the unlock button. By the time I exited our patrol vehicle, I was at least half block behind Officer Gil.

Even with the problems I had getting out of the car, I was able to catch up to Officer Gil and run past him as if he were standing still. I eventually caught up to the eighteen-year-old suspect, tackled him to the ground, and cuffed him. By the time Officer Gil and others got to my position, the guy was already handcuffed and ready to be transported back to our holding area for pre-booking. Officer Gil and others praised my actions. After we booked the suspect for numerous felony charges for causing one of our officers to crash during the pursuit and also being in possession of stolen properties, we went back to work. We spent the rest of the shift going from call to call. It was a very busy shift like Officer Gil predicted. I knew after that adventurous night that I wanted to become a full-time officer. I just loved the job and the camaraderie that came with it.

For my actions on this night, Officer Gil wrote a "Good Job" card and had other officers sign it. Soon, people in the department knew about me. There were many other nights like as I stayed a reserve officer for an additional two years. I had so much fun and loved what I was doing for South City.

I would come home and tell Joy and my mother of all the exciting things I got to do with South City. Joy and my mother didn't think it was very exciting. My mother, especially, would always tell me she was afraid I would get hurt. She said she always asked God, the holy spirits, and our ancestors to protect me from danger.

Passing of My Dearest Mother

TO ME, MY mother was the best mom on this Earth. Ever since that fateful night when she gave birth to me in that taxicab, she has always been there for me. If she could not be there with me physically, she would always be with me in spirit. She was a sweetheart and one of the nicest, most loving, and compassionate person that I have ever known.

I was her permanent fixture in the early years in Vietnam. Wherever she was, I would be right next to her. Some of my earliest and fondest memories were of her being the first person I saw after waking up from a nap. She always greeted me with a smile and a nice ripe guava. Throughout all the years that I was living with her, she would get up earlier than I would and ensured I had a nice home-cooked meal to eat, and her cooking was better than any restaurant food I'd ever eaten. When I got sick, she would always take care of me better than any nurse could. Whenever I had a fever, she would hold my hand or place a cool washcloth on my forehead to calm me down and make me comfortable.

As a kid, I thought my parents were crazy. Sometimes they didn't make any sense to me. After I became a parent myself, I understood why they acted the way they did. There are no words that could describe my gratitude for all they did for me and my siblings. I understood that being a parent does not end when our children become adults. We are parents forever, but it's the good kind of forever. From the day our children are born, we become parents for life! Even when our children leave for college, we will worry about their health and well being as long as we live, no matter how far away they are.

Every day of our lives, parents wonder about our children's future, pray for their health, and wish for their happiness. We will not hesitate for a moment to give our life for theirs if it is required of us. Parenting is the toughest job in the world today with different types of activities and issues abound. On any given day, we could be at multiple events for our children. My parents did their share of running around for us.

My mother also taught me the value of respect and tolerance for all people regardless of their race, ethnicity, religion, age, or sex. Respect is something that is sorely lacking in our modern world. She taught me that I am no more important or less important than any other being in this world, and that has served me well in life. It helps keep me humbled, while at the same time giving me a sense of self-worth. She was one of the happiest people that I knew, and she always seemed to have a smile on her face. I'm getting teary-eyed just thinking about her. My heart is full to the brim with love for her still today.

In early 1997, my mother developed abdominal and back pain. We had no idea what was happening to her. Even my mother did not know why she was having these painful episodes in her stomach area. She made numerous hospital visits, but her doctor could not figure out why she was hurting. Her doctor thought she had an ulcer, so he treated her for that condition unsuccessfully. She started losing her appetite and soon she began to lose weight. We kept bringing her to her doctor, but after numerous tests, they still could not figure out what was wrong. Her doctor referred her to a specialist who ordered additional tests to see if he could pinpoint the problem and help ease my mom's pain.

One day, her doctor called and gave us the saddest and gravest news ever. He told us one of tests for my mother came back positive for pancreatic cancer. He was not sure how much time she had to live. He scheduled for an immediate exam to determine what stage her cancer was in. I did not know anything about pancreatic cancer until my mother was diagnosed with it. The only thing I remembered about the disease was one of the stars in Little House on the Prairie, Michael Landon, had died from it in the early 1990's. I was so devastated that I could not finish my dinner that night. The rest of the family got together in the following days and went over plans how we would help our mother fight this disease.

Her doctor determined the cancer had spread to over half of her intestines and surgery was needed immediately to remove the infected part. After half of her intestine was removed, she felt somewhat better. She could only eat small portions of food at a time. Shortly after her surgery, Joy and I brought her home to our house so that we could take care of her. After a few months, she had no pain, so we thought she was going to be okay. She enjoyed living with us and being able to bond with Briana and our newborn daughter, Brittany. Joy would cook for the family, and I would help keep my mom's room clean. Every day after work, I would spend as much time as I could with my mom. I would sit there and just talk to her and tell her how much I loved her.

Then the day we all dreaded the most came. My mother's stomach pain returned. This time it was very severe. We brought her back to see her doctor. They did more tests and the test results confirmed our worse fear. The cancer had returned, and this time it spread to other organs inside her body. Her doctor said the cancer had spread too fast and that there were no treatment options available to save her life. Our entire family was so devastated by this new reality that our mother was going to pass on soon.

The doctor told us my mother would need someone to take care of her twenty-four hours a day and he recommended a hospice in Palo Alto. For the last month of my mother's life, she was unable to eat anything. She also required huge amounts of morphine to keep her pain tolerable. The great and caring people from this hospice helped me and the rest of our family through those last few weeks with kindness and dignity. I took time off from work and spent every minute I could with her. The last couple of days of her life, she was in and out of consciousness. My sisters and brother visited her daily, but I would stay with her throughout the night. I would sleep on the small chair they had inside her room. I heard her every pain and her every struggle for breath. The evening before she passed away, she asked me to tell the nurses not to try to save her when she stopped breathing. She said she was tired and it was time for her to be with my father. I held her hands tightly as she told me how much she loved me and that she was very proud of the man I have become. She said she was extremely proud of her son. I cried uncontrollably. There was this terrible sadness deep inside my heart that could not be explained. It was like she knew her time was coming.

On April 9, 1998, at 2:35 a.m., my mother took her last breath and shed one last tear from her right eye as I sat there crying uncontrollably. I felt this great sadness beyond my comprehension. I wanted so badly to start performing CPR on her to bring her back. But then I remembered her last wish of not wanting to be saved, so I just hugged her tightly. It was a moment in time that I will never forget. At least my mother did not die alone that early morning. I know my mother is now with my father in heaven.

She was one of the most amazing people that I have ever met, and I will always cherish every moment that I had with her. Thank you mom for all that you have done for me and shared with me. My life has been greatly sculpted by your influence, and it is all for the better. I am so happy that I was given a chance to be her son. If I could live up to her example in this life, then I will die a very happy and content person.

After the demise of my dearest mother, I decided to become a full-time police officer for South City. It was March 1999. Since I had already gone through a rigorous background check in 1997, they only completed a short update background check on me. I was sent with four other new hires from South City to the police academy at the College of San Mateo. We trained for six months on various police-related topics. By the time we were done with the academy, we had logged in eight hundred hours of training. We lost about one-third of our classmates during the way. However, South City did not lose anyone during the academy. We started out with five, and we finished with five. We graduated from the academy in August 1999, one month after the birth of our third daughter, Braelyn. We started our field training program shortly after. Police work is not for everyone. After being around police officers for a few years, you see the people that go into police work and are able to tell if it's a right fit. You could tell right away by their demeanor and work ethics if they are not cut out for this type of work.

I spent the next seven years at South City as a police officer. During that time, I came across many different unique situations, controversies, racism, self-discoveries, sadness, life-and-death situations, and much more.

There were many nights when I patrolled the streets of South City while its residents slept. While driving around, some times in very dark alleys, I felt a great sense of responsibility to the community I was serving. All of these folks depended on me and a few of my coworkers to keep them safe, protect their properties, deter crimes, and apprehend law violators if the need arose. I felt a sense of duty. A duty I owed to the community when I took my oath of allegiance and swore to serve and to protect the people. I felt a sense of courage. The kind of courage to take on the greatest villain of all without any fear I might get hurt while doing so. I felt a sense of selfless service to my community—to put the people's best interest before mine. These were some of the things that went through my mind at three o'clock in the morning as I patrolled my town. These were some of the things that motivated me to get out of my patrol vehicle and walk the neighborhoods. These were the things that motivated me to stop and talk to the people I served and listen to their problems. And not just listen, but come up with solutions on how to solve their issues. These were the things that made me a police officer. These were the things I love most about police work. There were other things that made my job a little more challenging, but then again, being a police officer I knew that came with the territory.

For example, I have made many car stops and have contacted many folks who claimed I pulled them over based on their ethnicity. I once pulled over an Asian guy who said I pulled him over because he was Asian. Say what, sir? I am Asian, too. How about I pulled you over because you didn't come to a complete stop at that stop sign? Or when I stopped a car that had all its windows tinted at eleven o'clock at night, the driver called me a racist and accused me of pulling him over because he was Hispanic. Say what, sir? I couldn't even see who was driving the car because the tint was so dark, let alone determined what race you were before pulling you over. There were many more of these similar encounters during my time at South City, and yes, I was not alone in coming across these types of incidents. My coworkers who are white police officers get accused of this tactic far more than I did. What I have discovered over the years was that some people will use any and every excuse they could come up with to not accept responsibility for their actions. It was not only certain ethnic groups that were coming up with these excuses. It was everyone that was doing it. It was never because they did something wrong; it was always the police pulling them over because of their race or because we had to meet our quotas. We did not have a quota system at South City.

There was this one time when I responded to a "grab and dash" from a liquor store in downtown South City. I just happened to be in the area and saw the kid run out of the store. I gave chase on foot and eventually caught up to him. I had him trapped in a dead-end street, so he stopped, turned around, and started talking trash to me. There is no respect at all for police officers here in this country. I was thinking back in Vietnam or in some other country this kid would probably get a spanking for being disrespectful to law enforcement officers. Here they knew there was nothing we could really do besides arresting him for the crime. The kid went on and asked me, "Are you going to kick my ass now, Jackie Chan?" I was taken aback a little by this remark. I thought about it for a second before being a wisecrack myself and asked him why did I have to be Jackie Chan? Why couldn't I be Bruce Lee? The kid laughed a little bit and said, "All right man. You got me." He even turned around and placed his hand behind his back without me even asking him to do so. His take? A bag of chips and some gum. It wasn't a good day for him.

I have seen plenty of dead people during my time at South City. So seeing a dead person did not bother at all. But the toughest moment was when I responded to a Sudden Infant Death Syndrome (SIDS) call in the Westborough neighborhood around four o'clock in the morning. I was the first to arrive on scene. When I first heard dispatch put out the call over the radio, I was praying that the fire department would get there before I did, but that was not to be. I went up into the fourplex townhouse complex and met the parents at the front door. Dad was crying and holding a lifeless body of a six-month-old baby. Mom was in the standing next to Dad screaming uncontrollably. Neighbors were out and about because of all the commotion. Dad handed the baby to me and expected me to perform miracles. I grabbed the baby from him and performed CPR. I tried my hardest, but I knew the baby had already left this world. The body was cold to the touch and lifeless, but I couldn't stop doing CPR. The parents were pinning every hope on me to bring their child back as they sat there and watched my every breath I gave to the baby and every chest compression I administered. I, too, was hoping for a miracle. I was hoping to start that little tiny heart again. I tried and tried, but to no avail. I continued to do CPR until our fire department personnel arrived. They took over, but they too were not successful in reviving the baby.

They "pronounced" the infant shortly after. The parents hugged each other in terrible pain as they tried to make sense of this terrible sadness. As part of my job, I had to inspect the infant's room to ensure there was no foul play involved. As I walked into the infant's room, there were pictures of the baby everywhere. The room felt very warm and full of love. Things were very neatly placed in all the right bins and the crib was especially clean. I looked inside the crib and noticed there was an empty space on a blanket where the baby had been sleeping. My sergeant arrived shortly and helped me go through the rest of the room and other places inside that house. We did not see anything that would make it a suspicious death, so we treated it as a SIDS case. We tried to comfort the parents, but there was nothing else that we could do. We left our business cards and asked them to call us if they needed anything. The husband thanked us for trying and appreciated our efforts.

It hit me especially hard because I have young ones at home. I couldn't imagine having to go through something that tragic with one of my kids. I couldn't even begin to feel the pain the parents were going through nor would I ever want to.

Some of the other things that affected me more than others included sexual assaults against children. I couldn't stand those heinous crimes. I often asked myself after those investigations, how can someone do that to a child? What got me the most was that most of the perpetrators were family members. It just makes me sick to the stomach to even think about that. I often had to be professional while dealing with these sick people during my interviews so that I could obtain their confessions. I wasn't sitting there talking to these sick folks because I wanted to make them my new friends. I did because I had to. There were times when I just wanted to reach across the table and hurt them. To let them get a taste of what it was like to have total trust in someone and have that person turn around and betray your trust and then end up hurting you. These innocent children never asked to be robbed of their innocence at such a young age. I couldn't reach across that table or else, I would not be a police officer anymore.

Other times when I responded to domestic violence incidents and find out some of the victims had been victims of violence for a long time, but won't do anything about the situation. At first, I did not fully understand the cycle of violence or how some of these perpetrators were really good with using children as a tool to keep their victims in the relationship or economic abuse, or other coercion techniques to continue to get away with the offenses. A perfect example was when I responded to a domestic violence call where this Thai lady had been physically abused for years. The only reason why we found out about this time was her neighbors heard her scream and called the police. When I interviewed her, she said it was in her custom back in Thailand to be physically punished for not being a good wife. She explained that every time she was late in making dinner for her husband, he would slap or punch her in her stomach. Most times she would try not to make any noise fearing that he might get madder and hurt her further.

This time her husband punched her too many times, and she could not bear the pain of being punched repeatedly, so she screamed. While I was talking to her, I could see the years of pain and abuse etched into her face. She seemed tired of the marriage and not having discovered happiness in her life. I made sure I told her that it was not okay to get abused like that here in this country and that there were laws against this type of abuse. I helped her with resources so that she could get help and get out of this nightmarish relationship. I gladly arrested the husband and charged him appropriately according to our laws.

There was not always the bad stuff that I came across during the course of my time at South City. There were many good people in South City—people that went out of their way to help others; coworkers who would not hesitate to go into the dark alley or through that door with you; coworkers who will be by your side when you find yourself in a life-or-death situation. I went through a life-and-death situation myself with Officer Toscano in 2003.

On the late afternoon of May 12, 2003, Officer Toscano and I showed up for work. We were working swing shift from 4:00 p.m. to 2:00 a.m. that day. We were assigned to work beats Four and One, respectively. These beats were usually very busy, because they covered the downtown area and the east side of our city. The areas downtown were some of the roughest neighborhoods in South City. This was where most of the gang members resided and where the less fortunate also live.

The day started like any other work day would. We showed up for briefing. We checked out our patrol vehicles before hitting the streets. Nothing was weird about this day. Everything appeared normal as they come, or in the police world, "routine." We drove downtown and conducted a few rounds of security checks at the parks, banks, and alleyways before heading to our favorite burrito place, Los Compadres, on the 100 block of Grand Avenue.

Officer Toscano and I got a snack to hold us down until dinner scheduled for later on that evening. We really enjoyed this place because the food was always delicious and the folks were always friendly to us. We left the restaurant telling ourselves not to create any unwanted work for ourselves for at least an hour to allow our food to digest. It seemed as if we had just jinxed ourselves by saying that. Officer Toscano and I were known to be the most pro-active officers in our department at the time. Officer Toscano drove to his beat while I went to mine. Our beats were right next to each other, so we were never that far from each other.

A few minutes later, I was traveling northbound on South Linden Avenue when I noticed a gold colored station wagon speeding in front of me. I got behind the vehicle and paced it over a one-fourth of a mile going thirty-five miles per hour in a twenty-five mile per hour speed zone. Instead of looking away, I initiated a traffic stop. I broadcasted my traffic stop over our radio so that other police units would know what I was doing. I could see that there were two people in the car at the time. The vehicle pulled over on the corner of Linden Avenue and Third Lane. I immediately exited my patrol vehicle, but so did the driver and the passenger. I ordered the driver to return to his vehicle, but he passively refused. The driver immediately started walking back toward my patrol vehicle while the passenger walked away from their vehicle.

Because of officer safety reasons, I focused on the driver and let the passenger go. I ordered him to return to his vehicle, but he kept asking me what he did wrong to get pulled over. He was very polite and kept saying, "yes, sir," "no, sir." Based on my training and experience, when a person is that polite to a police officer, that usually means that the person had been in prison before, so I asked him right away which prison he got out of. He had this puzzled look on his face and I knew right away that I hit the nail on the head. I told him to come stand on the sidewalk so that I could obtain his information. I explained to him why I stopped him, and he apologized profusely for speeding. He said he was in a hurry to get home and that was the reason for him to be speeding. By this time, Officer Toscano had pulled up and stood by as my cover officer.

There were a few things that I wish I could have done better during this traffic stop. The guy gave me a false name when in fact he was a Parolee at Large (PAL) and was considered armed and dangerous by the California Department of Corrections (CDC.) The false name he provided to me actually came back to another parolee. This crook couldn't even lie. I started to tell him I need to conduct a search on his person per the terms and conditions he agreed to when he chose to be paroled. He started getting squirrelly on me. He began walking backward while asking me to cut him a break and also to allow him to go tell his girlfriend who was supposedly at some store down the street he was being detained.

I told him he needed to stand still, turn around, and submit his person to be searched. Before I could do anything else, he took off running eastbound down Third Lane. Officer Toscano and I gave chase. I caught up to him approximately fifty yards later and tried to grab him from behind. This guy was about 5'10" weighing roughly 150 pounds and was really fast. I did not know how I was able to catch up to him in that short distance, but I guess when my adrenaline was pumping, I ran a lot faster. Officer Toscano was a little further behind us.

As I tried to grab the back of his shirt, he swung his right arm back and dislodged my grip. We continued to run eastbound on Third Lane. I initially put out over the radio that we were in foot pursuit, but I don't remember me providing dispatch with any more updates until we got to the fence line of a property fifty yards later. At this fence line, I grabbed him and was trying to bring him to the ground. For a guy weighing roughly 150 pounds, he put up a ferocious fight. He was throwing punches and elbows at my head in an attempt to knock me out or at least off him. I was blocking some of his punches and elbows, and at the same time I was trying to wrap my arms around him to throw him on the ground.

At some point, I slipped and fell to the ground. He was standing over me and I saw him dig deep into his right pants pocket. This was not a good sign for me being at the position of disadvantage. I knew right away he was going for a weapon, but I did not know what kind of weapon he would pull out. I screamed out, "He's going for a weapon. He's going for a weapon" in order to alert Officer Toscano.

Sure enough, as I was getting up off the ground the guy pulled out a black compact handgun and began pointing it at my head. We were only a foot or two away from each other. I did not have time to think about anything at this point except to try to create some distance between him and me. I quickly pushed him away from me. As I was trying to unholster my duty weapon, a 40-caliber

Berretta, I could see him pointing that gun at my head. I could not even begin to describe the horrifying feeling that came upon me at this point.

My life was flashing right before my eyes. I would never be able to see my daughters grow up or be able to kiss my wife again if I was to die today. I could still remember vividly the way he was holding the gun. He had it in his right hand. He had it tilted with his palm facing downward (gangster style.) Then he fired one shot. I don't remember if I heard it, but I knew he had fired by the way his hand jerked back. That day was one of the luckiest days in my life. He missed! As he was about to fire again, Officer Toscano arrived in the nick of time and shot at the guy, but for some reason Officer Toscano missed all four shots he fired. Officer Toscano saved my life that day. If he had not gotten there in time to shoot at the suspect and scare him off, the suspect could have possibly got a second shot off, and might have been lucky the second time. Thank God for Officer Toscano's timely arrival.

The suspect then ran along the fence line trying to get to Third Lane. I had my duty weapon out and was ready to engage the suspect. Officer Toscano and I ran after the suspect. I got to the corner of Third Lane and the entrance into a parking lot before the suspect did. I stopped and pointed my weapon at the suspect and ordered him to drop his gun. He was approximately twenty-five to fifty feet from me. The suspect refused my order, raised his gun up, and fired a second shot at me. Lucky for me, he missed again. I fired two shots at the suspect and he was hit by both. He went down immediately. From my vantage point, I could see he had been hit in his left arm and in his left-buttock area. As Officer Toscano and I approached him, we could see the black compact handgun two feet from his left hand. I quickly kicked it away from his reach. He was pleading for help.

He kept asking for me to call him an ambulance because he was bleeding. There were so many thoughts that went through my mind in a matter of seconds as I got to where he was. I remembered I was very, very angry at him for trying to kill me and Officer Toscano. I was relieved that the shooting incident was over, and I was glad that Officer Toscano and I were going to go home safely that night.

After we handcuffed him, I did call an ambulance for the suspect. As much as I did not want to help the guy immediately after I shot him, the cop inside of me returned. He was arrested and transported to the local hospital, where he was treated and subsequently booked into our county jail. Officer Toscano and I went through a series of interviews from within my department and also from the San Mateo County District Attorney's Office to ensure the shooting

BRIAN HUYNH TRAVIS

was justified. Many witnesses were tracked down by our detective bureau and interviewed. After a long court process, the suspect was found guilty by a jury of twelve men and women. The suspected was sentenced shortly after to seventy-five years to life for the attempted murder of me and Officer Toscano. He was also a two-strike felon, so he won't be getting out of prison anytime soon.

Every so often, I still think about that fateful afternoon. I still think about the fact that if the suspect had just aimed his gun at my head the way we were trained to shoot a weapon, then he would have hit me that day. I wouldn't be around to see my children grow up or grow old together with my wife. I often thank the Lord for protecting me and Officer Toscano that day. Officer Toscano and I became lifelong brothers after the ordeal. I was glad I went through it with him. Things happen for a reason. God put people in your life for a reason, and I am glad God put me with Officer Toscano that afternoon.

We moved to Fairfield in 2000, because our family had expanded and we needed to get a bigger house to accommodate our family of five now. We found a perfect home in Fairfield and moved in November of that year. We lived across the street from my brother and sister-in-law and their two children. Our two families would often get together and have BBQ's. My brother-in-law, Tom, is a police officer with the San Francisco Police Department. Tom is a very good person and we get along really well.

After moving to Fairfield, I started commuting with my buddy Mark whenever we ended up on the same shift together. Mark lives a few cities east of me, and he commutes all the way to South City. That is an hour-and-a-half trip each way with no traffic, and perhaps a two-hour trip with traffic. I don't know how he does it. He said he loves working in South City and would rather commute than work anywhere else closer to his house. We did try to sign up on the same shift every year so that we could commute together. Not only commuting together saved us money and wear and tear on our vehicles, but it also gave us time to become better friends. We would do really crazy things to each other to pass time or to keep each other awake after our graveyard shifts during the long ride home. Mark used to wait for me to fall asleep on the way home after a graveyard shift and he would pour water on my pants, or he would put lipstick on my lips. He was a greatprankster.

There were many other coworkers at South City that I have gotten really close with. These were my brothers and sisters from an extended family when I was away from home. The brotherhood and sisterhood of police work that we all cherished and want. We used to get together after the shift for a beer. We played softball together. We partied together and when someone had a big project at home, we all pitched in and helped get it done. Our families would get together on weekends and have BBQ's and swimming parties. We know our buddies' wives, husbands, and children by first names. I was brought up in a police generation where if you were new, you sit in the back of the room and keep your mouth shut. When it was time to choose your patrol vehicle for your shift, you let the "seasoned" folks have the newer cars and you drive the ones that the city was about to retire. After 2001, the department hired younger adults that did not know the police culture, or they simply just didn't care because of their generation and how they were brought up. These younger adults often played video games throughout high school and were awarded a trophy regardless if they won or lost. These were the same kids that think they don't die because in the games they play, they get unlimited amount of lives.

Some showed up brand spanking new out of the academy and think they know everything. When the "seasoned folks" correct them on things, they get offended. Others who made it through their field training programs felt like they were instant veterans. They felt entitled to sit toward the front of the room or wanted to drive the newest patrol vehicle we had in our fleet. On the streets, they acted and felt like they were back playing a game, like they were invincible with unlimited lives. We "old folks" took a lot of these newer officers and mentored them, so they could truly know what it was like to be in a brotherhood or sisterhood of police work. We successfully assimilated some while others were slowly getting it. Luckily for us, there was no real problem, child.

Things were going really well for me at South City. I was starting to feel comfortable with being a police officer now with five full years under my belt. I also went back to school and worked hard to obtain a Bachelor of Arts (BA) in Criminal Justice Management from the Union and Institute University in Sacramento. Everything was falling into place as far as me moving up the ladder at South City. I had the time and experience as a police officer and now I had the civilian education. I was primed to be promoted, but then my career and my family life had to be put on hold as I went to go serve in our nation's Army.

L to R—Mother, brother Thai, Brian, sister-in-law, sister Tan, in Phantiet, 1971

Brian standing with his father and mother in Phantiet, Vietnam, 1973

L to R – Brian, sister Tan, nephew Tuan, and brother
Son, Phantiet, 1973

Brian posing for a photo in Phu Hai, 1975

Brian with his sister, Binh, at the refugee
camp in Indonesia in 1979

This apartment complex in San Mateo was where Brian, his sister and
brother first lived after they arrived in the U.S. in 1979.

Brian in sixth grade at Abbott Middle
School, San Mateo, 1982

L to R – nephew Peter, sister Binh, father, Brian, nephew Tuan,
mother, at Lake Tahoe, 1983

Brian and Gary at Tim's house in the San Mateo Village in 1984.

L to R: Binh, nephew Brian, his mother, sisters, My and Tan, nephew Patrick and his brother, Son

Junior yearbook picture in 1987

L to R—Mzao, Mike, Brian and Shane. They were
a very formidable 4x100 relay team. This team won many meets
during the 1987 track and fields season.

Senior football picture in 1988

Chris, Brian and Rey, hanging out in Foster City, 1989

Brian's boot camp photo, 1993

LT Tealdi, and CPT McCracken pinning the badge on Brian at
the South San Francisco Police Department, 1997

Brian and his mother in 1998, just a few months prior to her passing.
By now she has lost a lot of weight, as was evident in this picture.

Brian and the rest of his family at his mother's rosary.

Operation Iraqi Freedom, Iraq, 2004-2005

SOMETIME IN MAY 2004, our battalion had drill for the weekend. We were conducting training at our armory in San Rafael. I was talking to a fellow Guardsman, First Lieutenant Laughlin, at our armory about the rumor of our battalion getting called up to support the ongoing Operation Iraqi Freedom. The rumor was that we would be activated sometime in August or September to train up at Fort Lewis, WA, for a few months prior to going into Iraq. At the time, I was a First Lieutenant, and Bravo Company's Executive Officer (XO.) Our company commander was given time off for this training weekend, so he was not there. I decided to go speak to the battalion commander, Lieutenant Colonel Wells, to put this rumor to rest once and for all. He was in his office at the time and he was not talking to anyone. He told me to come in and close the door. I asked him if the rumor was true about our battalion possibly getting called up for Operation Iraqi Freedom. He looked at me for a second, possibly thinking about whether he should confirm the rumor or just tell me something else. After a second or two, he told me the truth. He said our battalion was next on the rotation from the State of California to go support Operation Iraqi Freedom. He has not seen anything concrete yet from higher-ups that said we were going for sure. Before I left his office, he told me I might not have to go if our battalion got called up because I had just come back from a deployment to Bosnia, but he could use a leader like me to help him in Iraq.

I remembered leaving his office feeling very conflicted. I had just come back from a nine month tour to Bosnia as part of Stabilization Force Rotation 14 (SFOR 14.) I was with a small contingent of soldiers from our battalion that deployed with the Minnesota Army National Guard from August 2003 until March 2004. Our small contingent did many amazing things while we were deployed on that mission. For most of us in that group, the Bosnia call-up was our first "real" deployment on foreign soil. Being away from my family was always tough. I remembered there were many nights in Bosnia where I wished I was at home with my family. I realized I was soldier and I had a mission to do, but it was still hard when Thanksgiving and Christmas came and went without spending on single moment with my family I didn't get to read my children Christmas stories or see their eyes sparkle as they opened their presents on Christmas day. I missed my wife's, Braelyn's, Brittany's, and Briana's birthdays because of this mission. I started feeling sorry for myself and for my soldiers toward the end of our deployment, but then I started thinking about all of the brave men and women who fought during World War II and also in other protracted conflicts and I realized how some of them did not get to see their families for years, if at all. That made me realize our deployment was not that bad after all. We were in a permissive environment in Bosnia, and no one had ever shot at us during the entire deployment. I sucked it up and drove on and completed my mission.

Bosnia had a completely different situation than that of Iraq. It was a peace-keeping mission. The Bosnia Conflict pitted three ethnic groups against one another. The Bosnian Serbs, the Bosnian Croats, and the Bosnian Muslims all fought against one another and committed genocide against each other. Thousands died and about half the population was displaced. Neighbors fought neighbors. Most towns and cites were destroyed. Bosnia-Herzegovina's people were left impoverished and traumatized. We were there to help its people rebuild their country and also to keep the peace at the same time.

Iraq, on the other hand, was thought to have a connection to the hijackers that attacked our country on 9/11. They were thought to have weapons of mass destruction, and now they were full of Al-Qaida operatives and Iraqi insurgents trying to kill us and destabilize the country. This was a real war. This was something I had been training the past eleven years for and that was to go to war and fight for my country. I also wanted to give the people of Iraq a chance at democracy. After thinking about everything, I no longer felt conflicted. I knew exactly what I was going to do if our battalion were to be called up for the Iraq mission.

That night I came home, but I did not say anything to Joy and my children. I didn't want them to be worried already about me leaving again. It had only been two months since I came back. Our family was slowly getting back to being normal again, so this news would really upset them. I thought I would wait until our battalion actually got the mobilization order before I say anything to them.

A month or two passed by without any word from higher-ups that our battalion was getting mobilized. Then at our July drill, Lieutenant Colonel Wells called all the leaders in our battalion into our conference room and broke the news to us. He confirmed that our battalion had just received the mobilization orders and we were supposed to travel to Camp Roberts in August to complete pre-mobilization tasks. Then in September, we were scheduled to leave for Fort Lewis, WA, to conduct additional training up until we left for Kuwait, and then into Iraq. He also told us that our unit was put on stop loss, meaning no one could transfer out or leave because of the stop loss order.

I remembered walking out of the meeting with my mind going a mile a minute. It took me a few minutes to process everything. There were a million questions that went through my head. Was I ready for the biggest challenge of my life? Could I do it? What if something were to happen to me while I was over there? Where were we going? What was I going to tell my employer? Would this deployment affect my promotion chances at South City PD? How was I going to tell my family that I was going? I thought about how my family was going to take it. I came back to my company and called for a company formation. There I broke the news to them. Everyone had the same look I had when I walked out of the conference room. Since it was toward the end of our drill weekend, I released them early and told them to go home and spend time as much time with their family as they could.

That night I came home and broke the news to Joy and my children. I could tell Joy was not very happy, but she wanted to be supportive. That's what I love most about her—that unconditional support when it comes time for me to help our country. She reminded me that Iraq would not be like Bosnia and I needed to be extra careful. I promised her I would take good care of myself and my soldiers.

For the next month, I spent every available minute I could with my family. I read a book every night to my daughters before they went to sleep. Time spent with them was very precious to me and to them at this point.

I also informed, Chief Raffaelli about my future deployment to Iraq. He too was not very happy that I was leaving again, but like Joy he was supportive of the deployment because he knew our country was at war. He told me to let him know if I needed anything while I was over there. I thanked him for his understanding and support.

For that August drill, our battalion traveled to Camp Roberts to complete our pre-mobilization tasks. We arrived Friday night and got ready for what we knew would be a long weekend. Our battalion was not at full strength at the time, so many soldiers from different units throughout California got orders to report to Camp Roberts to also go through the pre-mobilization process with us. Those who met the standards would be augmented into our battalion and deploy with us. Those who did not meet the standards would be sent back to their units. The next day we went through a slew of medical screening stations, trying to determine who could be deployed and who was unable to deploy due to injuries. We stood in line for hours at a time to get through the administrative stations. They wanted to make sure our military and civilian paperwork was in order. At the end of that day, we were told Lieutenant Colonel Wells wanted to address the entire battalion regarding our impending deployment.

We assembled in a dining facility that was not being used at the time. Lieutenant Colonel Wells officially gave us a quick timeline of our mission and all the tasks we needed to complete before going to Iraq. He also spoke to us about how important it was for soldiers to go help fight for our country and that we have trained for this chance at combat. There were some in that room that expressed excitement about the deployment. However, most of us had too many things racing through our minds to show any kind of a reaction. As I looked around the room, I saw many different kind of soldiers sitting there listening attentively that day. I saw a few grandmothers, many grandfathers, parents, brothers, sisters, uncles, aunts, nephews, nieces, grandsons, granddaughters, strangers, hard workers, not-so-hard workers, Asians-Pacific Islanders, African Americans, Caucasians, Hispanics, Middle-Easterners, folks from India, and many others from many different corners of the world. We were all in this one room at this moment, preparing to fight for America. I asked myself, "Why, America? Why are we all here and willing to fight and die for her?" I had an idea why, but I did not fully understand the true meaning of "why" until I was halfway into my deployment in Iraq. For now, I was just happy and proud to serve our country.

After the meeting, Lieutenant Colonel Wells began interviewing the folks that had just returned from the Bosnia deployment to see if we would be willing to go again with the battalion on this deployment. Lieutenant Colonel Wells had spoken to two captains before he got to me. They had refused to go with us for reasons that Lieutenant Colonel Wells could not discuss with me. Lieutenant Colonel Wells started our meeting by telling me I was one of the best lieutenants in his battalions and he would love for me to take command of Bravo Company when we deployed to Iraq. I was thinking to myself, "Sir, you didn't even have to hang a carrot out there for me to go. I was going to go anyway," but giving me command of Bravo Company was definitely a huge bonus. I told him I would go with the battalion into battle and would love for the chance to take command of Bravo Company. Lieutenant Colonel Wells thanked me for my patriotism to our country and told me Bravo Company would be mine to command.

It was a great honor to be given the responsibilities and trust of those above and under me. For me, it was a duty of service; I serve the Soldiers in my company. Without them, I was just another individual. I think leadership is one of the greatest honors of all, probably because it is one of the greatest challenges any person could face. That was the reason why I decided to get my commission. I wanted the opportunity to lead and inspire Soldiers. They really do become your family. They can frustrate you at times, but in the end, they will always be a direct reflection of you. To know that I was going to war to keep my country and our people safe, there was no greater satisfaction. I knew there would be many rough days in Iraq and nothing there would come easy. I also knew in my heart that at the end of the tour, I would be able to look back and be proud and understand what we did over there.

I left that meeting a very proud soldier and a very proud American. I would have never dreamed that one day I could get a chance to be a commander of a U.S. Army Company when I nearly died on my boat journey while escaping from Vietnam twenty-five years ago. I thought to myself that only in America was this dream able to come true.

The medical and the administrative screenings conducted all weekend did weed out a few soldiers that were not fit or ready for the deployment. By the end of the weekend, we had a pretty good sense of who would be going with us on this mission. The soldiers who passed their medical and administrative screenings were told to report to our unit for the September 11 to 13 weekend drill. We were supposed to finalize a few more things and tie up all loose ends before we traveled to Fort Lewis on September 24. I was put on orders prior to September 1 in order to get a headstart with the planning. I still had to complete a change of command inventory with the outgoing commander, meet with my new First Sergeant, 1SG Gunnerson, and my Operations Management Team (OMT) OIC, First Lieutenant Laughlin to go over my expectations with them. I also had to meet with my supply sergeant, SGT Burgos. I was a very busy person during the first half of September.

Time with my family became more and more precious as we neared our departure date for Fort Lewis. Instead of reading one book to my daughters every night, I would read two or sometimes three. Instead of giving them one or two good night kisses, I would give them ten or more. My embraces with Joy were much longer and tighter. Our nightly talks would be a lot longer than usual and "I love you" was said more often to each other.

The battalion staff was also put on orders for the first week of September to prepare for the deployment. At our armory in San Rafael, leaders would have daily planning meetings. Lieutenant Colonel Wells finalized his battalion staff with Major McEwing as the Executive Officer (XO); Major Elliott as our Operations Officer (S3); our battalion supply OIC (S4) was First Lieutenant Dee; our battalion Security Officer (S2) was Captain Murari; CPT Cardozo was the Administrative Officer (S1); and First Lieutenant Mooldyke was our Signal Officer (S6). The company commanders were CPT Prasad for Headquarters Company; CPT Chan as the Alpha Company Commander, and myself as the Bravo Company Commander. Our battalion was to link up with the 525th Military Intelligence Brigade (Airborne) from Fort Bragg in Kuwait and be under their command for the Iraq mission.

Our mission in Iraq was very complex. We were to interrogate enemy prisoners of war, conduct counterintelligence and long-range surveillance. This was a mission that was among the highest priorities in Iraq since U.S. and Iraqi troops struggled for intelligence on a shadowy opponent in a battle that had killed more than fifteen hundred U.S. service members at the time (2004) and untold thousands of Iraqi civilians. However, it was also a controversial mission, in the wake of the Abu Ghraib prison scandal, in which military police and intelligence officers stood accused of abusing Iraqi prisoners.

Our higher command was well aware of the controversy and had us go through training in permitted interrogation methods, the Geneva Conventions, and the rules of war. We were to get additional training on these topics at Fort Lewis.

I was in command of sixty very qualified and motivated soldiers. I stressed to them that we needed to focus on the mission at hand and encourage our families to do the same. Soldiers face nothing in combat more dangerous than distraction from worries at home. I told them to concentrate on doing their own jobs right rather than worry about others who had done theirs wrong. I was not too worried of our soldiers misbehaving, because most of these folks were a lot more mature and older than the ones that were involved in the Abu Ghraib scandal.

On Thursday, September 23, 2004, we had our farewell ceremony at the Lagoon Park, next to our armory. It was a beautiful sunny day. There was a slight breeze in the area and nearby were many pond ducks frolicking in the water. There were 137 soldiers that lined the field that day. Many were nervous, some filled with anxiety, and others were scared. There were many more family members that came out for this special farewell ceremony. We barbecued chicken under a cerulean sky. We shared some laughter and shed some tears. We hugged and kissed our families carrying red, white, and blue balloons. We tried to reassure them, but their hearts were full of worries. Lieutenant Colonel Wells told the crowd that day the 250th Military Intelligence Battalion was making, "a journey into history, to a war-torn country where they will witness battle and building, occupation and if all goes well the first free Iraqi elections." Lieutenant Colonel Wells continued with, "Lord, look after our families. Tomorrow, we will catch our flights and we will begin our journey." It was a very moving speech.

Shortly after Lieutenant Colonel Wells' speech, fathers, mothers, sons, daughters, grandparents, one by one would come up to me and ask me to take great care of their loved ones and to bring them all back safely. I reassured them I would do everything in my power to ensure they would be safe during their missions. But how can I promise to bring everyone back safely? There was no way I knew I could keep that promise. Not in Iraq, and not based on what we were going to do. We were not a company that was going to stay on base and do paperwork. We were a company that had to go outside the wire and face insurgents, Improvised Explosive Devices (IEDs) and other dangers on a daily basis to talk to people and collect intelligence so that we could help the field commanders win their battles on the streets of Iraq.

After the farewell ceremony, we said farewells to our families and went back to getting prepared for our departure the next morning. It was very hard saying bye to my family, but I knew we would get a three-day pass to see them again prior to deploying to Kuwait, so it made our good-byes more bearable.

Pre-Deployment Training at Fort Lewis, WA

THE NEXT DAY we traveled by commercial air to Fort Lewis. We arrived sometime in the early afternoon and were transported to the "Old North Fort" where our male soldiers were assigned building number 11D59 and our female soldiers were assigned building number 11D60. It was cloudy that day. I have been to Fort Lewis a few times before during annual trainings with different units over the years. There was very little to do on this part of the base. There was a gym and a dining facility nearby, but other than that, there was not much to do. There was only one coffee place on North Fort, the "Battle Bean," which we all loved to visit each morning before the start of the day.

Fort Lewis was where I met my admin sergeant, SGT Jones, for the first time. She was the most qualified admin sergeant in our battalion, but for some reason she was not needed in our battalion admin section, so she was given to Bravo Company to help us with our admin issues. I was very fortunate to get a person of SGT Jones' caliber and experience.

There is a U.S. Army policy that mandates every company appoint at least one individual to document the unit's activities during wartime. It was a very easy choice for me to make. I selected SGT Jones as Bravo Company's historian. We sat down and spoke at length about her new duties and her background. The more I knew about her, the more I was impressed with her dedication to her family and to our country. She is a loving wife, mother of two daughters, and a twenty-year veteran who will be dedicating herself to recording and preserving the knowledge gained by Bravo Company during Operation Iraq Freedom III.

SGT Jones believed everything in this war would be a learning experience for every soldier, airman, sailor, and marine, and the Bravo Company experience will someday help future companies involved in conflict operations. SGT Jones, who is a 42A Military Occupation Administrator, was mainly tasked with processing and ensuring that all unit and personnel documents were in order.

Military history is the recording (in writing or otherwise) of the events in the history of humanity that fall within the category of "conflict." This may range from small disputes between two tribes to mad dictators inciting world wars. It teaches us that every war is unique, delineating what tactics, techniques, and procedures were effective in past conflicts.

Unit historians not only document major events and operations, but also provide insight into how soldiers lived and died and the weapons and technology they used during times of conflict. Many great commanders have benefited from strong foundations in military history. General George S. Patton, one of America's great tacticians, was an avid reader of history. He studied tactics intensely, learning much about potential adversaries. As early as 1909, while still a cadet at the Military Academy, Patton wrote in his personal notebook: "In order for a man to become a great soldier . . . it is necessary for him to be so thoroughly conversant with all sorts of military possibilities that, whenever an occasion arises, he has at hand, without effort on his part, a parallel. To attain this end . . . it is necessary . . . to read military history in its earliest and hence crudest form and to follow it down in natural sequence, permitting his mind to grow with his subject until he can grasp, without effort, the most abstruse question of the science of war because he is already permeated with all its elements."

I believed through historical records to be kept by SGT Jones, and others like her, during times of conflict, future soldiers and military officers can gain a valuable base of knowledge in the art of war, enduring the security of the United States through continued success of the U.S. military efforts worldwide.

After our meeting, we went back to work preparing for our mission. Our first week at Fort Lewis consisted of going through the Soldier Readiness Process (SRP), receiving uniforms, boots and field equipment from the Central Issue Facility (CIF), attending a slew of mandatory briefings, receiving many shots (Anthrax shot #1 included), testing our protective masks in the gas chamber, and conducting many Common Tasks Training (CTT) in our barracks. In the military, there is no free time. If we were not busy completing SRP tasks, we were preparing for war. So what did that mean for the Soldiers in my company? Training, training, and then more training! Which meant classroom time and physical training whenever possible, but it's not always your run-of-the-mill classroom instruction. This was the time we give responsibility to our junior Soldiers and promote their development into leaders. For example, my 1SG might assign them a class to teach or give them a task to accomplish. This was also a very important opportunity for us to evaluate soldiers in anticipation of those future operations in Iraq. As leader, I always stress to my junior leaders our jobs should never take a backseat. We need to always lead from the front, and we always need to lead by example.

We knew that the training we were receiving at Fort Lewis would probably be one of the most important trainings of our lives. Our success in Iraq would hinge on how prepared we were for that one chance, since it only took just *one*.

October came very fast. We had been training nonstop since our arrival at Fort Lewis on September 24. The days were long and the nights were short. During our time at Fort Lewis, our day began at 5:00 a.m. for Physical Training (PT) and ended sometime between 9:00 and 10:00 p.m. I tried to give my soldiers time to relax from time to time, but those were far and few in between our busy schedule. The other thing I had to watch out for was the flare-up of seasonal affective disorder (SAD). This is a disorder caused by the lack of being in the sunlight during rainy or winter season. Fort Lewis is located in the state of Washington and it seemed like it rained every single day that we were there. After it rained for twenty or something straight days, everyone was starting to feel the blues. My 1SG and I started to observe our soldiers' energy declining a little, a decrease in creativity, being less social and more irritable among one another.

This was not an isolated phenomenon in my company. It was also happening in HHS and Alpha Companies. My 1SG and I got together with the other company leaders and decided to approach Lieutenant Colonel Wells to see if we could give our soldiers a day off to rest and re-energize our souls. Lieutenant Colonel Wells understood the situation and agreed to give all soldiers in our battalion a day off. This was on October 16 and it was our first day off, some twenty-three days after we arrived at Fort Lewis.

Though it was just one day off, it did us a lot of good. Most of us spent time getting some extra sleep while others attended to their personal issues. We started back up again the next morning. We went through live fire exercises, got our second Anthrax shot, went through lanes training, and then more lanes training. On October 27, we received our third Anthrax shot. Our battalion had a barbeque toward the end of October and we were given a day off to travel to Seattle. Seattle was great, but there was a light sprinkle that day. What else was new? It had rained, drizzled, or misted over 90 percent of the time we were there. Yet these mists, drizzles, and rains keep Seattle cleaner and greener than most cities of a similar size. Most of us visited Pike Place Market, while some ventured to the Space Needle. We all had a great time and some much needed R & R.

Before we knew it, November had arrived. The first two weeks of November were very important to us. Not only were we required to finish the administrative part of our SRP, but we had to go through two days of convoy live fire lanes. I did not want any accidents or mishaps while we were at these lanes. I didn't think anyone else wanted any accidents or mishaps either. I have to admit the first day was very scary for me. We rode in the back of the deuce-and-a-half truck and fired live rounds at stationary targets. In the back of my deuce-and-a-half truck were a couple of soldiers that lacked experience in handling the M16 weapon system. So instead of concentrating on my targets, I was watching them to make sure they handled the weapon and engaged their targets properly. Fortunately, we all got through these two days unscathed.

We got our two-day pass on November 12 and 13. My wife and kids flew up to see me for the last time before we left for Kuwait. We spent every minute and every second together. I hugged my family as much as I could and there were plenty of kisses to go around for everyone. We went downtown Seattle and visited many places. We really had a great time. My girls were clingy, because they knew that Daddy was going to war and fight for our country. They also feared that their Daddy might get hurt. I reassured them I would take real good care of myself, and I would see them again in a year. Saying goodbye was always the toughest part. My young ones did not want to let go. We did a group hug and just held on for as long as we could. I tried not to cry, but that did not work. We were all crying at the end.

Shortly after seeing my family off at the Seattle International Airport, I got back to Fort Lewis and went right back to work. We completed every step required of us from the SRP staff. We received additional equipment issues from CIF and began packing all of our things into our connexes for shipping.

BRIAN HUYNH TRAVIS

Getting Ready in Kuwait

ON NOVEMBER 16, we completed the packing of all duffle bags and cleaned our area. The next morning, we turned in our linen and vacated our barracks. That afternoon, we were driven to McCord Air Force Base for our flight to Baltimore, Maryland. We arrived there on November 17 at 0100 hours, local time. We departed Baltimore at 0300 hours and arrived in Germany on November 18 at 1640 hours, their local time. We were exhausted, but there was still the last leg of this travel. We got a two-hour break to stretch out and relax a little before we boarded our plane again. We departed Germany at 1915 hours and arrived in Kuwait on November 19 at 0205 hours, local time. We were bused to Camp Doha for mandatory briefings shortly after our arrival. After the briefings, we were bused to Camp Virginia and Bravo Company was assigned to Pad 7, tent #1.

I was so tired that night that I went right to sleep. I did not get a chance to see the entire Camp Virginia until next morning. We got up early that morning, but we did not conduct physical training. I wanted to give my soldiers some time off so that they could get some extra rest from the two days of travel we just did. My 1SG and I walked to breakfast. While walking to the dining facility, I looked around and noticed Camp Virginia was a mixture of tents, prefabricated buildings, supply yards, metal buildings, and barracks. The sand there was the finest I have ever seen. It was light brown in color and could easily be kicked up into swirling clouds. The wind could blow up without warning and just as quickly diminish. There was very little vegetation there. I saw some dust-covered bushes, but that was about it. I saw some sparrows chirping and flying quickly between buildings. It was a long walk from where our tents were to the dining facility. Once we got closer to the center of the camp, we could see flags from the countries representing the forces that were stationed there for their deployments. There were soldiers from South Korea, El Salvador, Great Britain, and the United States.

Once inside the dining facility, there was a wide variety of food available, but it's the same selections every day with very little variation. The workers appeared to be mostly from India and the Philippines. If you did not like to eat in the dining facility, then there was a cluster of fast food restaurants nearby. There were also a few shops, an Internet café, the gym, Welfare and Recreation Center (MWR), and a chapel. We decided to dine in the facility instead of spending money on fast food. This was a very noisy place. Generators of all sizes provided the electricity for the entire camp, and they could be heard all over the camp like white noise. There were air conditioners rumbling in every building and every shop.

After we ate, we returned to our tent area and went over our schedule for the next week and a half at Camp Virginia. From November 20 until November 29, we spent all day training and firing different weapon systems. Our Tactical Human Intelligence Teams (THT) received additional specialized training while others qualified to drive LMTV trucks and up-armored Humvees. It wouldn't be complete without mandatory briefings on rules of engagement and weapons safety violations. We met with our 525th Military Intelligence Brigade Commander, Colonel Fant, a day or two after we arrived in Kuwait. The 525th Military Intelligence Brigade was a regular Army Unit from Fort Bragg, North Carolina. At first I did not know how Colonel Fant and the rest of his staff would view us, since we were National Guard soldiers from California. I thought he would treat us guardsmen differently, but that was not the case. Our command staff met him and his staff in the brigade headquarters' tent. They all seemed pretty high speed with their airborne patches and badges. Colonel Fant was very professional and even wanted to let us, know that he had a lot of respect for the soldiers in our battalion because we bring so much work and life experience to the table. That was a very true statement. In our battalion, it seemed like the average age for our soldier is approximately thirty years while our active duty comrades seemed a lot younger.

Colonel Fant and Lieutenant Colonel Wells went over the details of where they wanted to place my THT teams. I was to place two teams in An Najaf, two in Karbala, two in Al Kut, and two in Ad Diwaniyah. My company headquarters and I would also be at Ad Diwaniyah. They told me the entire Central South Iraq was very active prior to our arrival, so we should expect to see some action during our deployment. I was concerned, but I knew I had good soldiers in my company and if we did everything by the book, we should come out okay. Our meeting lasted a few hours before we went back to training.

Our days were long, but the nights came quickly in the desert. There was no lingering twilight like back home. When the sun set, it became completely dark. We slept on cots the entire time we were in Kuwait. Our bathrooms consisted of Porta-Potties that were located fifty meters from our sleeping areas. We showered in converted cargo containers that often had long lines during peak hours. The amenities weren't the best, but they weren't the worst either.

Before we knew, it was time to fly into Iraq to start our mission. On my last night in Kuwait, I treated my company to pizzas and sodas. We shared much laughter and spent a lot of time reflecting on the last three months of training hoping it would be enough to get us through the year-long deployment. We prayed together as a company and hoped God would watch over and protect all of us from danger. We trusted we would be in His good hands.

Operation Iraqi Freedom Begins

I LEFT THE safety confines of Kuwait the next morning along with Lieutenant Colonel Wells and a few others on the advance party into Iraq. Our flight into Baghdad International Airport (BIAP) was very uneventful, and that was how we liked it. I got off the plane and looked around and it was surreal. I was now standing on Iraqi soil. I was in a real war zone. This was not Fort Lewis, Bosnia, or Kuwait. My brethren were dying here on a daily basis. There were real insurgents, Improvised Explosive Devices (IEDs), and folks with real Rocket-Propelled Grenades that were ready to kill us in the blink of an eye and without prejudice. I didn't realize it, but the more I was thinking about the realities of Iraq, the tighter my grip on my M16-A2 became. I was scanning in all directions, looking for any possible trouble, but there was none that day.

Soon the folks that we were replacing arrived at BIAP and picked us up. They were from the 502nd Military Intelligence Battalion. They took us to their headquarters located in Camp Victory and introduced us to their battalion commander and the rest of the staff. We spent the next few days receiving briefings and also acclimating to being in Iraq. We were staying in the temporary tents just a few miles away from the headquarters. I had a chance to take a quick tour of Camp Victory while waiting for the rest of my company to arrive from Kuwait. The first thing I noticed right away was a complex of caramel-colored stone palaces that were inherited from Baath Party strongmen. One of these palaces was named, "Al Faw Palace." There was a food court that included Pizza Hut, a Subway, and Burger King. Nearby, there was a coffee shop and a Laundromat. There was a huge gym and two PXs centrally located. There were also two dining facilities. The food in these dining facilities was so much better than that from the dining facility at Camp Virginia. They even had an ice-cream bar inside each dining facility.

There was a swimming pool in the Australian soldiers' housing area. I walked by and saw people in the pool while others sunbathed nearby. If I wasn't lugging around my 9-mm pistol and my M16A2 rifle everywhere on Camp Victory, I would think we were at a resort in Las Vegas. Life on Camp Victory was not bad at all for being in a war zone. But deep down inside, I knew there was no way other camps around Iraq had all the array of modern conveniences and amenities like Camp Victory, and I was right as my time in Iraq went on.

The rest of our battalion arrived a few days later. I briefed them on what our plans were and how our company headquarters would support them during our mission. I went over what I was expecting from each and every soldier in my company. The next few days, we went over many briefings and last-minute training. I also allowed my soldiers time in between training to go check out Camp Victory and use some of its amenities before we went to our forward operating bases (FOBs.) On December 12, our counterparts arrived at Camp Victory and escorted us back to our respected FOBs to start our year-long mission. Soldiers in my company knew that it would be weeks before we could all see each other again, so we exchanged handshakes and hugs before departing the safe confines of Camp Victory to our FOBs.

Our company headquarters section and two of my teams arrived at Camp Echo unscathed. I was surprised we were not ambushed with small arms fire or IEDs during our trip from Camp Victory. Our counterparts were really excited to have us there. They were counting down the days until they could get out of Iraq. They told us many stories of all the things that happened while they were there. Living space at Camp Echo was very limited, so we had to share sleeping quarters with the outgoing unit for the next two weeks. The outgoing unit was supposed to show us everything we had to know about Camp Echo and our area of operation for one week. Then they were supposed to step back and watch us to make sure we were doing everything correctly before they could be released to go back to Camp Victory and, then to the good old USA.

Camp Echo is approximately 180 kilometers south of Baghdad. It was the forward operating base in the Multi-National Division, Central South area of operations. Camp Echo was also home of the Polish Army's 25th Air Cavalry. There were approximately fifteen hundred Poles stationed there during this time period. There were also other allied soldiers stationed on the same post such as the Bulgarians, Romanians, Ukrainians, and others. Life on Camp Echo was not bad though most of us would rather be home. Although the camp offered fewer amenities and was on a smaller scale compared to Camp Victory, it boasted more features than what we were expecting. We had access to free laundry services, an Internet café where it was relatively cheap to use, a phone center, a small PX, an Iraqi coffee shop, Morale, Welfare and Recreation Center, and a gym facility.

The soldiers lived in containerized housing units with beds, electricity, and air conditioners. Most of us arrived with the expectation of living in tents for at least a short period of time, but that was not the case. There was a good-sized dining facility that served a variety of food. Most of the workers are from Southeast Asia.

Before the sun rose each day over Ad Diwaniyah, the predawn silence was broken by the muezzins' calls to prayer, bellowing from electric loudspeakers throughout the city. For us, the new day began much like the last. We assembled outside buildings made from mud and clay to go over the day's mission. Others bustled about inside, performing the often tedious but always essential administrative tasks that keep our unit's many programs and operations in motion.

I knew my job would get a lot tougher very soon as I had teams at Camp Lima in Karbala, at Camp Hotel in An Najaf, Camp Delta in Al Kut, and Camp Echo in Ad Diwaniyah. Besides being very involved with our company's day-to-day missions, I had to ensure all of my soldiers got their mail from their loved ones from home and other essential supplies.

In order to do this, my company headquarters support team would have to travel to each camp on a weekly basis to deliver the goods. During this time, the roads in Iraq were often laced with many deadly roadside IEDs and vehicle-borne IEDs also known as VBIEDs.

The insurgents' weapons of choice against United States and allied forces during our time in Iraq were with IEDs, Rocket-Propelled Grenades (RPGs), and small arms fire against coalition truck convoys. These tactics employed by the insurgents were nothing new. Insurgents have found that truck convoys have been excellent targets since the 1950's when the Viet Minh attacked the French along the "Street without Joy." With that in mind, I made sure none of my company convoys would leave the FOB with "soft skin" vehicles. The vehicles had to be hardened wheeled vehicles so that they could protect our drivers from roadside blasts and small arms fire. The hardened wheeled vehicles would give my soldiers the necessary protection so that they could keep going to get out of the kill zone.

The other thing I wanted to ensure happen was every one of our Tactical Human Intelligence Teams (THT) had to have a strong security team to be part of the convoy to intimidate the enemy and provide overwhelming fire power in the kill zone. Each THT team usually went outside the wire in a three-vehicle convoy, so I directed there would be at least two gun trucks in these convoys.

After two weeks of training, our counterparts determined that we were ready to take over our area of operation and start our mission. The outgoing company commander wished me luck before pulling his entire company back to Camp Victory. Now we were on our own. Our THT teams went right to work on collecting intelligence and our headquarters company support team began roaming the streets of Iraq to support the company. Since we were so short on bodies, I had to go on every single convoy. Each week, we went to each FOB at least once or sometimes twice depending on mission requirements. The FOBs were not close to Camp Echo at all. Camp Delta was the furthest away with travel time ranging between two to three hours each way. Camp Hotel in An Najaf was approximately fifty-five minutes away. Camp Lima in Karbala was the closest and that was at least forty minutes each way with no issues. There were times when we were on the road seven days a week. It took a toll on our bodies physically sitting in those up armored Humvees day in, day out, sometimes in 120-degree temperatures. It was also very taxing on our psyche, not knowing when your convoy would be attacked next.

A Day in a Life of a Company Commander

AFTER ABOUT ONE hundred convoys or so, it all just felt the same to me. I got used to the idea that every convoy or combat mission I go on might be my last. I was not afraid of dying. I figured if that was God's plan for me to go, then so be it. I didn't let it worry me to death, no pun intended. It was around May 2005. I fell into a daily routine. My day would start like this. The alarm clock would go off at 0430 hours in the morning, and it's time for me to get up. On most days, the wind, a melodious hum, would pound against my trailer. It would play a familiar but exhorting tune. I reached over and turned on my light. Usually exhausted from a mission the day before, I get myself to crawl out of bed. Most of the time, my body lobbied to stay in the prone position. I would subdue the temptation and usually make for my water bottle or a cold premade Starbucks Frappuccino from my small refrigerator, like a child reaching for a favorite toy. I usually down the whole thing. I throw on my uniform, and rush outside to the nearest portable bathroom to brush my teeth. From May until late September, the oppressive heat, like a sledgehammer, usually hit me in the face as I started my day. Most of the time, the temperatures would reach eighty-five to ninety degrees before five o'clock in the morning. I began each day by praying for my family back home and also for the soldiers under my command, asking God for another uneventful day through the *Highway of Death* in the *Land of the Disenchanted*.

I would turn my thoughts to the tasks at hand, slowly inventorying the tools of my trade: a Colt M-16A2, a 9-mm Beretta, a 10-inch dagger, a Motorola radio, my helmet, my body armor, grenades, ammo, my Iridium Phone, maps, my military ID, my dog tags, and a picture of my family, and my two dogs. I usually head to the motor pool and account for my troops and watch my soldiers conduct their pre-combat inspections, starting with the radios and gas tanks. They check the machine guns: *mounted.* Combat lifesaver bags: *stored behind the passenger seat.* Straps: *tied down.* Fluid reservoirs: *filled to right levels.* Shooters: *focused, combat-ready, bladders empty.*

At 0530 hours, my convoy commander, SSG Taylor, gathers everybody for the safety brief. My soldiers know it by heart. They've heard the convoy briefs numerous times. Some lip-sync with SSG Taylor. He would tell them, "Seventy convoys in Iraq will be hit today. The odds of us being hit by insurgents this exquisite day are less than 5 percent. However, it's probably a great idea to stay alert". After his briefing, I give them ten minutes and then give the order to mount up. We drive to the clearing barrels—an area designated to load or clear weapons—lock and load and prepare to go out the wire. We normally would make our first stop in An Najaf, a holy city for the Shia muslims of Iraq. We would go out the main gate of our FOB and hook a left. Najaf is a fifty-five-minute drive. We drive through the arid environment until we near the city, crossing the ancient Euphrates. The soil around this mighty river is some of the finest in the world for growing crops. Date trees sprout like wild mushrooms.

We watch people work their fields as An Najaf appears upon the horizon. We go through the city during the early hours—the streets and the marketplace are devoid of people. Another ten miles and we hit Camp Hotel. Our soldiers at Camp Hotel rush our vehicles. The convoy is the bringer of morale—we have their mail and other essential supplies. The temperature climbs. It is now 0715 hours, and 100 degrees. We leave our vehicles and look for shade. Sometimes we pick up a couple of soldiers for transport to Baghdad. Departing Camp Hotel, we head for Camp Victory located near the Baghdad Airport. Our route takes us back across the Euphrates, over Bridge Road, down Highway L, and through Al Hillah. Babylon, the cradle of civilization, is only a mile away. There, in the *Land of the Two Rivers,* the Arabs created the earliest form of alphabetic writing and algebra. We go past the American Embassy sitting behind stonewalls and rows of concertina wire and catch Highway J. Sweat poured down our faces in rivulets.

The temperature usually reaches about 110 degrees by 0900 hours. We cruise down the highway doing fifty-five miles per hour, as our vehicles struggle to maintain our current speed. We slow to forty-five, so we don't blow an engine—bad news if you're outside the wire. We cross the last checkpoint before entering the Triangle of Death. With over one hundred missions under my belt, the many things I've seen are what you see on TV or read about in the papers. We dodge animal carcasses and abandoned cars which are favorite hiding places for Improvised Explosive Devices (IED.) While driving on the highways of Iraq, our convoy maintains a middle-of-the-road posture to avoid bombs. We avoid guardrails and permit no one to pass us, unless they're Coalition Forces. Any other vehicle could be a vehicle-borne IED (VBIED).

That includes the Iraqi Police and Iraqi Army because insurgents have stolen their uniforms and vehicles. We go past Highway I, once known as "the most dangerous road on Earth." Twenty minutes later, we enter the protective embrace of Camp Victory. We have just spent the last four hours in a rolling sauna, soaking all our clothes. The quickest route to comfort is to shed those clothes. We pull up to the clearing barrels and watch each other tear off body armor like it was ridden with plague. The relief is immediate. But our wet clothes stay on, drying slowly as the moisture evaporates. Salt residue snakes all over our uniforms, like cracks on a crumbling wall. We proceed to Battalion Headquarters to pick up supplies and drop soldiers off. In four hours, we will leave Victory's sanctuary and return to B Company's Headquarters in Camp Echo. Another two-and-a-half hours of utter discomfort, enervating monotony, tar-sticky sweat, and real danger that is so deceivingly far, yet so faithfully close.

BRIAN HUYNH TRAVIS

Ferrara Pan Candy Company Donated Treats for Iraqi Children

DURING OUR DEPLOYMENT, we received many care packages and support letters from a lot of caring people back home. The Ferrara Pan Candy Company did their part in supporting the troops and made a lot of Iraqi children happy by sending us Lemon Head candies. It all started when our company communications specialist, Specialist White, received a care package full of Lemon Head candy from home. He began handing out Lemon Head candy to children who lived near Camp Echo and to those waving on the roadside as Bravo's convoys passed by. Out on a convoy one day, he spied a little child outside Camp Echo's gate and gave the child some candy. The child was overjoyed, touching a chord in Specialist White's heart. The next week, he saw the child again, waving an empty box of Lemon Heads at the convoy, signaling for more. Specialist White knew that he had to get more. He contacted the makers of the confection, Ferrara Pan Candy Company and spoke with their representatives, Alyssa and Maria, to order more. The company did not deliver to APO addresses, but upon hearing the story, the company was so touched by Specialist White's gesture, it decided that if ever there would be a time to make an exception to policy, this would be it. The company *donated* several cases of the treat, in apple, grape, and lemon flavors and shipped them to Iraq. The kids were happy, but none happier than Specialist White himself. Thanks again to the Ferrara Pan Candy Company for their support and generosity.

Letters from Children at Laurel Creek Elementary School

T HE CHILDREN FROM Mrs. Brust's Kindergarten/First-Grade class from the Laurel Creek Elementary School in Fairfield, California, sent us pictures of themselves and much more. My wife was volunteering with the Laurel Creek PTA and became good friends with Mrs. Brust. When she heard I, along with other soldiers from California, were in Iraq, the gracious teacher and her eager young charges sent us care packages containing photographs, seasonal confections, greeting cards, drawings, handmade gifts, and letters. Our soldiers received many of these items before letters from their own families, bringing a bit of sunshine to otherwise dreary days. One package that was extremely well received contained an assortment of drink mixes, flavored tea, and gourmet coffee, with a letter explaining that the contents were for warming our hearts and minds. Around Easter, the kids sent Jelly Bellies, handmade cards, and drawing of rainbows (to make our living spaces more colorful was the explanation!)

In the summer, we knew school was out and thought that the packages would stop arriving. Were we mistaken. The kids surprised us with sunscreen, socks, cookies and small packets of crackers. To show our deepest appreciation, I sent her class a California flag, signed by the soldiers in my company. Mrs. Brust and the children asked our soldiers to become pen pals. The curious, young minds asked amusing, and sometimes heartwarming questions, such as: What does it look like? Where do you live? Where do you sleep at night? What do you do each day? What do you have to eat? Do you know any Iraqi children? Do they have a school near you? What do you need that we can send you? Many soldiers took time out to pen a few words to the kids. Our friends include: Joey, Nicole, Natalie, Mercedes, Gabriele, Jason, Darius, Christina, Dallas, Christian, Dakura, Arielle, Anazja, Bryan, Briana, Cameron, Teeannan, Audrey, and Samantha. So dear Mrs. Brust, thank you again to you and your wonderful children for sending us your little packages of caring, and drawing those splendid rainbows, and to all you generous parents of these fantastic kids, thank you from the bottom of our hearts. You made the miles not nearly so many, and the hours not nearly so long.

South San Francisco Police Department Dispatchers

Sent Treats

I WORKED AS A police officer for the City of South San Francisco for about seven extraordinary years, and that entire time, I have had the pleasure to work with many professionals and caring colleagues and supervisors at the department. The remarkable people I know are too numerous to mention by name, but there are two whom I simply cannot overlook: our dispatchers, Christine and Marianne.

I have known Marianne since we were freshmen in high school—quite a long time ago!—and I worked with her for at least six years. She is the kind of person who will do anything for anyone. You don't even have to ask; her heart is huge enough to sense that you need something! I have known and worked with Christine for the last seven years. She is an astonishing person, one who will, with no hesitation, sacrifice for the well-being of others.

After hearing from my e-mails about how soldiers in my company needed some Kool-Aid to make the water taste better and how the Iraqi kids near our base camp loved the candy our troops tossed them, Christine and Marianne wasted no time in putting together a care package drive for the troops. The support was overwhelming. Christine and Marianne received donations from coworkers, fellow police officers, dispatchers, and fire department personnel. Remarkably enough, even strangers gave their support. The St. Gabriel Elementary School in San Francisco was an inspiration, with kids writing letters and sending packages. The people of our community gave so generously. The San Mateo County Times helped greatly by publishing an article called *Dispatchers Rally Effort for U.S. Troops,* written by their staff writer, Emily Fancher.

At the end of the article, Emily listed the address and phone number where Christine and Marianne could be reached and where packages could be dropped off. After the efforts of our two big-hearted lady friends, we received well over one thousand care packages! These ladies spent countless hours of their own time, making incalculable personal sacrifices to mail the packages to our troops in Iraq. I can't imagine the extent of the workload involved—it must have been tremendous. We will never be able to repay them and we don't even dare to. I could not accurately describe the emotional highs of the lucky recipients of these packages, our troops, and the Iraqi children. What resulted from their painstaking labors was the palpable gratitude of our soldiers, so far away from home and battling the despair of solitude, and of the kids, so distant from the luxuries we in the western world know only as conveniences.

When I sent Marianne and Christine an e-mail thanking them for their thoughtful gestures, their reply, humbling in its utter simplicity and disarming in its bottomless humanity, was, "That's the least we can do. Thank you for fighting for our country and helping to keep us safe in America." Christine said, "At first, people drove around with American flags on their cars, but you don't see that anymore. The devastating news (of U.S. soldiers dying) in Iraq makes people feel helpless, but this small gesture can comfort those abroad and here. It's like a piece of home is there."

Bravo Company 125th Convoy

BEFORE WE KNEW it, summer was upon us, but for soldiers in my Company, we didn't have a nice stroll at the beach to look forward to that summer. No iced lattes at Starbucks, no cold beer at a sports pub. Instead, we conducted combat patrols and convoys through the streets of Iraq in 120-130 degree heat. We would squeeze into uncomfortable Humvee seats for hours, jarred by vibrations of the vehicle's tank-like diesel engine and transmission. We would be in a fatiguing, mind-numbing, hyper-alert status, searching for roadside bombs and sniper sights. We would do it again and again and again.

On June 8, 2005, Bravo's resolute soldiers did their 125th mission. Before the deployment is over, we would do a 160 more. Mostly in the Central South Iraq, occasionally through the "Irish Car Bomb" alleys of Baghdad, but always in those claustrophobic armored Humvees. They will trek with weapons at the ready and their comrades at their sides. The convoy teams vary in mission, size, and capability and their common thread is the bond each soldier has for the other. Wartime comrades are a hard wearing breed. They talk tough to one another, but the concern they have for each other often surpasses family affection. They have no choice. Their lives depend on it.

It's a blessing that we were able to travel through the most dangerous parts of Iraq and return to our camp without any casualties or major injuries. Specialist Godina, who was a former Los Angeles sales associate, wanted to become a police officer. One day she told me that she was getting a lot of practice in weapons handling so she should be ready to take on the tough streets of Los Angeles. Specialist Godina was the only female turret gunner in the battalion. The convoy usually passed debris of vehicles destroyed in roadside attacks and other dreamlike situations that could easily turn nightmarish.

We were surrounded by a deadly environment. We were shot at numerous times. We drove through war zones. We had debris and rocks thrown at us. But we stayed motivated. We focused on the mission, but most importantly, we focused on each other. We didn't think about what may happen. We definitely have knowledge of what could happen, and we continuously trained and prepared for the worst.

Pre-deployment training, at home station, at Fort Lewis, and in Kuwait, has made a big difference in preparing soldiers for combat in Iraq. Combat patrols and convoy missions were not taken lightly. Briefs prior to departure cover numerous items, including weather, potential hazards, contingency plans, and intelligence. The enemy threat is the single most critical item that is discussed. The enemy lurks at every turn, every traffic stop, and every tranquil hamlet.

Many people have come together to ensure the safety of Bravo Company's combat patrols and convoys, and the hundreds more that crisscross Iraq's desert and urban environs, day in, day out. There are the dedicated professionals back home who built the vehicles, weapons, and various pieces of gear. There are the suppliers and manufacturers, the vendors and the clerks, and the legislators and the taxpayers. Bravo Company simply continued the tradition of military preparedness and mission focus.

On this very same day, an Improvised Explosive Device (IED) attack on a three-vehicle convoy from our sister battalion near Baghdad, cost the life of a fellow soldier. An American hero was called home that day. For his family, our kindest words cannot ease the pain of his passing. The memory of our brother, friend, and fellow intelligence professional will stay with us long after this deployment is over. The sacrifice that he made will not be forgotten, nor will it be in vain. Three other soldiers suffered serious injuries. One of the injured was originally from our Battalion, but was attached to our sister unit, to help out during the deployment. Everyone injured in the attack has recovered.

The tragedy of that day was great. I know that our nation will enjoy freedom for a long, long time because of the willingness of people, like our departed and injured colleagues, to give so selflessly of themselves.

Bravo Company Trained Iraqi Army

N O ONE WOULD have guessed it, friends and foes sharing a class room. Well, make that *former* foes and *present* friends. The scene is repeated many times across war-torn Iraq, when United States Army soldiers paired up with their Iraqi counterparts to provide instruction on an array of military subjects. That would include intelligence. On April 24, 2005, two Bravo Company soldiers had the opportunity to teach soldiers of the new Iraqi Army, the esoteric-sounding *Intelligence Preparation of the Battle field* or IPB. My OMT chief, First Lieutenant Laughlin, chose two very knowledgeable intel specialists, MSG Logue and Specialist Norton, from our OMT shop to go to the Numaniyah Iraqi Army Base. MSG Logue called it "two very rewarding" days where they shared their expertise on how to prepare the battle space from the intel point of view. MSG Logue told us, upon his return, that he really enjoyed interacting with the Iraqi Non-Commissioned Officers (NCOs). He said they are the future of the Iraqi Army.

Through two competent interpreters, a lawyer and a medical student, Bravo Company's soldiers presented not-so-easy technical material to their diligent student hosts. Consecutive translations of the information posed a challenge, since the instructors had to pause and wait until the "terps" completed the parroting of the lessons. The Iraqis provided a UAZ, a Russian cold-war-era Jeep, for the two instructors to drive while at the camp. Specialist Norton told us the Jeep was like "an Alabama roller coaster." After ten hours of instruction and two hours of review (and countless opportunities to intermingle), the staff officers and NCOs of the 3rd Brigade, 5th Division Iraqi Army puzzled over a practical exercise (PE.) Their knowledge was put to a test when the instructors required them to create graphic staff intelligence products. Specialist Norton told us that their apprentices started out slow, but when they got to the PE, they really got into it. They were really interested. But could they do it in real life? We assumed they would if they paid attention in class that was taught by real-life practitioners of the IPB craft—an American Master Sergeant and Specialist.

Bravo Company Maintenance Dream Team

A SOLDIER CANNOT afford a vehicle breakdown, where the environment was at best, shaky, and at worst, downright treacherous. Stuck in a hostile spot and vulnerable to a ferocious enemy whose only intent is to kill or capture U.S. soldiers was not something anybody wanted to confront. Perfectly functional and fully reliable vehicles were the key to ensure that situation did not come to pass.

I had the maintenance dream team of MSG Garcia, SGT Ernest Mulvey, and Specialist Casas. These three fine soldiers turned an abandoned building and an empty gravel lot into the best maintenance shop in the whole Central South Iraq. They single-handedly rebuilt the motor pool with sand bags and ringed it with barbed wire. They established two maintenance areas—a petroleum oil and lubricant area and a parts room. More importantly, forty major non-routine services on the company's vehicles were completed. This was no small task, considering that the Battalion's support services were in Baghdad, three hours away. They had a mind-set that believed no matter what the job was, they could and would get it done.

In recognition of these accomplishments, 525th MI Brigade Commander Colonel Fant, on his visit to Camp Echo on May 10, presented Brigade coins to the maintenance section's crew. I will be forever indebted for their service to Bravo Company's soldiers and our country.

"Old Timer" on Camp Echo

IN LATE JULY, I ran into a Polish officer whom I first met when I arrived at Camp Echo, Iraq, in early December 2004. At the time, he was getting ready to go home, in January 2005, after fulfilling his deployment obligation. After a six-month hiatus from Camp Echo, he was back for another tour. "Brian, you are still here?" he asked. It suddenly dawned on me that I have now acquired a label of sorts, that of "Old Timer." Most of the members of the Coalition Forces, American and European, and a few others from South America and Asia, who were here at Camp Echo when we first arrived, have since rotated out. Fresh troops arrived to take their place. New faces by the hundreds have appeared. My friend and I spoke for a little bit and said temporary good-byes. Later that day, I reflected on what had happened the past eleven months on active duty: from the two-month mobilization training at Fort Lewis, Washington, in September to November 2004, to our final preparation rehearsals in Kuwait, and finally to our arrival in the war zone of Iraq. I realized how long we have been away from our loved ones, and how divine it would feel when we finally see them again.

Everyday we hear of our brethren falling on the battlefield. It is a fount of terrible sadness, but also a wellspring of resolve. Every time we hear that another Improvised Explosive Device (IED) had been detonated, injuring or killing our friends and the innocent of this country, we feel the somber criticality of our presence. The daily tragedies impel us to get out there and do our jobs with stronger focus. We are driven to root out the insurgents who are trying—because of a perverted sense of self-importance—to destroy the dream of freedom that has eluded this society for half a century. We are driven to capture the purveyors of death and mayhem, plain terrorists who cloak themselves behind a perversion of a great religion. We are driven to find the caches of weapons these insurgents and terrorists use so that they will not have an opportunity to use those instruments against us.

As for my Polish friend, I bid him a fond farewell, and to see him again after that, either in sweet home California, where I live, or in the great country of Poland, where he lives, or in any other place, save for Iraq or Afghanistan!

Leaving Iraq

FINALLY! THE DAY came when we got our orders to return home to our loving families. Right before I left, I reflected on the last twelve event-filled months of our somber foray into the Iraqi Theater of Operations. I could not help but be touched by a pang of melancholy. I could still remember vividly on November 19, 2004, Bravo Company and the rest of the soldiers from 250th MI BN (TE) arrived in Kuwait, anxious to get on with the job in Iraq. I remember our soldiers saying, "Sir, let's get there and take care of business! Let's not spend too much time in Kuwait." We did spend time in Kuwait, keeping it to the minimum to complete certain requirements, and packed off to Iraq. One year has now passed since that unforgettable November day when we entered the unreal world of a real war zone. Bravo Company has not only done the job with the utmost expertise, but also we did it with just the right blend of élan and care. Most of what we do is classified and cannot be shared here. The restrictions of our job prevent me from doing so. We have accomplished things that make us stand out amongst the other companies in our entire Brigade. In a strategic sense, the tactical work that we did here has made a difference in our military's efforts to defeat the enemy and rebuild a nation.

Bravo Company was unique—perhaps reason enough why we were so successful. We had soldiers from the Army National Guard, Army Reserves, and Active Duty Army. We had soldiers from divergent slices of society, from different trades, from dissimilar educational levels, from the former dean of Southern Methodist University to a high-school graduate, from a salesperson to a police officer. We had veterans of real-world deployments, and we had fresh military-school graduates. We each contributed a thread that made our tapestry strong: life experience. We had the final ingredient that created chemistry: the work ethic of our proud soldiers. That ethic was so elemental to the whole mix that we didn't need to call too loudly when it came to our missions. We are where we are today because our soldiers packed that ethic into their duffels before trudging off to war, like a mason packed their square and compasses into their tool bag when they trudged off to build King Solomon's Temple.

The accomplishments of our soldiers were uplifting. Here are some examples: over two thousand mortar rounds, artillery shells, mines, and rockets detonated; over twenty thousand rounds of ammunition destroyed; and over 150 RPG-7V launcher tubes confiscated. The list is long, the contents lethal. I am truly proud of our soldiers. I could have not been any prouder.

Bravo Company's journey was over after one long and eventful year. To anyone who contributed to the renewal of the battered land of Iraq, that is a source of sadness. In my eyes, I see the faces of Bravo Company's soldiers, our gutsy citizen warriors, who volunteered for this mission and sacrificed so much to stabilize the fledgling democracy of Iraq. As the Company Commander for Bravo Company, I have had the precious opportunity of watching our Operation Management Team and our Tactical Human Intelligence Team develop, persevere, excell, and succeed under the most adverse of conditions. I have First Lieutenant Laughlin to thank for that.

Our teams were a microcosm of America. Tough Texans, fervent Floridians, well-rounded Washingtonians, and unassuming Utahans mixed in with our core group of convivial Californians. To describe them all accurately and faithfully taxes my linguistic skills! But one thing remains—I am very proud of what they have accomplished. I now see with greater clarity why America is as great as it is. We are a people united not by ethnicity or religion, but by the common belief in principles of freedom, individual worth, and human dignity.

I know that after Bravo Company left, Iraq would still be there. The conflict would not be over. Sadly enough, there would be more mayhem, more death, and more despair. Soldiers and marines, sailors and airmen will continue to pay the ultimate price for the flag they nobly serve. A burgeoning insurgency will continue to set back the machinery of progress. However, somewhere in Iraq's ancient landscape, a child will wave in awe at a passing U.S. convoy, and a new school will rise to illuminate eager, young minds. Somewhere in Iraq's arid terrain, a woman will vote for the first time in her life and raise her eyes from the shadow of her burkha. Despite the many troubles that we have encountered along that journey, Bravo Company will have left an imprint in this country, maybe not quite as towering as Mesopotamia's contribution to human civilization, but as indelible and historic nonetheless. That was our legacy.

BRIAN HUYNH TRAVIS

Back at Home

I CAME BACK home from the deployment, knowing it would take time to re-assimilate back into my family life. I thought I could just get back into the swing of things, but that was not the case. It was a trying time for me and my family during the first few months I got back. I found myself often short with my wife and my children. We would argue a lot more after I came back than before I left. My wife and I realized what was going on, and we would sit down from time to time and go over how we could make things better so the problems did not get any worse. It seemed to work because we argued less and less. I still find myself scanning all overpasses before I drive underneath them. I continue to want to exit the overpass in a different lane than the one I drove in. This was due to our driving tactics in Iraq to avoid insurgents hiding on overpasses, lobbing grenades down onto our Humvees as we exit.

There are four things that still stay with me up to this day. Those are the unfriendly stares we got from time to time while driving through Iraq; the stench of burning trash; the poverty of the Iraqi people; and the Iraqi children lining the roads as we drive by hoping for a piece of candy or a water bottle.

I was awarded the Bronze Star Medal and the Combat Action Badge (CAB) for my performance in Iraq. Those awards did not mean as much to me as bringing all my soldiers back alive. No award could ever top that.

I also came back to South City PD a different person. I did not realize I had changed until a few of my coworkers brought it to my attention. They kept telling me I was not the same guy. I tried my best to make it seem like I was the guy that never left, but that did not work. So I tried to make the best of it.

In December 2005, I initiated a name change to append "Travis" to my last name. The name change also affected the names of my wife and my children. This was a fundamentally life-changing decision for my family and myself, made only with the utmost of thought and the greatest of deliberation. The reason was simple, but reflective of the values we have as an American family, and a brief chronology will help explain both.

Right before I left for Iraq, I participated in cultural awareness class at South City. My colleagues and I learned much about one another, including backgrounds, family histories, values, and interests. I shared my own story of how as a young boy I traveled from a distant shore to the place I now call home, the United States. The time was the late '70s, and the country which I left was Vietnam.

It was a difficult time for my family. Vietnam was and remains Communist. I remember the atmosphere of oppression that pervaded, along with the numerous societal ills ancillary to it. My family made the crucial decision to escape by boat. It was a great risk, but one which we were willing to undertake collectively as a family for a shot at freedom and economic betterment. Surviving the high seas for thirty long days was a challenge, but our story ended happily when we landed on an Indonesian island and eventually contacted U.S. governmental agencies.

We availed—and I am eternally grateful for it—of the refugee sponsorship program instituted after the Vietnam conflict to assimilate the so-called "boat people" and other disadvantaged groups into American society.

It was in November 1979 that my family and I arrived at Travis Air Force Base. I can repeat with unabashed and proud candor that I kissed the tarmac of Travis Air Force Base after we disembarked the military aircraft that represented our final flight to a free and promising future. Travis Air Force Base was where my American life began. I was nine years old at the time.

Now I wanted to add Travis to my last name because it is my way of honoring the magnanimity of the country that took me in and to keep alive the richness of our family's severe, but storied past. My family discussed this idea, and we made this decision together. Travis Air Force Base is not just a geographical point on the map for us, but a place that will forever represent the goodness of the United States, the opportunities she offers to those willing to take them, and the largeness of the hearts of the American public.

Briana, my teenage daughter, thought it was remarkable how I de facto started my life at Travis, which by extension, started hers as well. She and I, and my entire family didn't want that story to fade over time. My family unequivocally shares this idealism. I wanted Travis to be my new last name, and I also wanted my family to perpetuate Travis in their names. It was my way of broadcasting to the world that I am in America's debt forever.

When I first told some of my Vietnamese friends I had added Travis to my name, they initially gave me a hard time and called me a "sell out," but after hearing the reason why I did it, they understood and actually supported my decision. Some of my coworkers at South City had mixed feelings about the name change, but overall most of them were very supportive and did not care what name I went by as long as I continue to go out there and fight crime and keep the people safe.

During the rest of my time at South City, I was able to work different assignments, different shifts, and I even worked a stint on the downtown bicycle program. I was selected to be on the SWAT team and went on a few "real" call outs. I made many lifelong friends while I was there.

In July 2006, I decided I could no longer work for the South San Francisco Police Department due to practical matters of the economic sort. The appallingly high gas prices and the increased bridge tolls that I have to pay daily, coupled with my long commute to and from Fairfield, pushed me to make that painful decision. I had wanted to finish my career at South City. I had spent nine years, which is a quarter of my life, working there. I was fortunate to have worked at the South San Francisco Police Department.

I got hired with the Solano County Sheriff's Office in August 2006. My commute now is five minutes. Ancillary, but no less important a benefit, is that I get to spend a lot more time with my family and be the father that I want to be for my daughters. They are growing up quickly before my very eyes and I want to be a part of those years.

Nine years is too long a time to catalog all the important, memorable, or life-changing events that happened to me while at South City. But I remember a few, which I wanted to share . . .

> . . . my first vehicle and foot pursuit with Officer Gil in 1997;
> . . . the officer involved shooting that Officer Toscano, and I had against a parolee-at-large in 2003;
> . . . the enormous support from all, everyone in the department, while I went away to serve in Bosnia and Iraq in our nation's army;
> . . . the practical jokes Officers Saunders, De Lacruz, and I played on each other;
> . . . the accidental bumping of CPT Massoni to the ground while chasing down a 459 PC suspect in the Costco parking lot . . .

I could go on forever with these great memories, but I will, for now, keep them in my mind and in my heart. Time will cloud the details, but the episodes and their effects on me, as a man, as an officer of the law, and as a member of our great fraternity of servants of the community will never be erased. I will cherish them, and think of them, and think of everyone that was a part of my life. It was nine wonderful, wonder-filled, and wondrous years. It was a heck of ride, and I am the better for it.

BRIAN HUYNH TRAVIS

Solano County Sheriff's Office

I BEGAN MY career as a deputy sheriff for the Solano County Sheriff's Office in August 2006. Being a deputy sheriff was a lot different than being a police officer for a municipal police department. At Solano, we patrol the rural parts of Solano County and your cover officer is a "minute" away, not like seconds at the South San Francisco Police Department. A "minute" does not mean sixty seconds. We are talking perhaps five to ten minutes of waiting time should you call for a cover officer. There are less of us on patrol, and we cover a larger area. My first day at Solano was very memorable. I remembered I was in the locker room getting dressed for work that morning when one of the deputies came up to me and introduced himself. I thought that was a very nice gesture. We spoke for a few minutes as he was trying to learn more about my law enforcement background. At the end of our conversation, he asked me something that really stuck to my mind and also put me on guard. He asked me if I had a "clique." I told him no. I had just gotten there. Besides, I was not into the "clique" thing. I am my own person and I did not feel like I needed to belong to a "clique." I believe in earning your promotion, or other commendations base on ones merit and not because you belong to a "clique."

This deputy advised me that the sheriff's office was a little more political than where I had just come from, just by the nature that the sheriff is an elected official and whereas the chief of police is an appointed position. I did not know what he was talking about until I had been there for a few more months. Yes, things are a little more political here, but the benefits of working near my home and having many good coworkers are so much greater than a few small drawbacks. The political game is everywhere. I quickly made many new friends and sprung right into action in a form of a Field Training Officer (FTO.) Since I came from a department that was pretty busy, I got to handle many calls for service, and through handling and investigating these calls, I gained a lot of experience as a police officer. When Solano asked me if I wanted to help train new deputies from the academy and pass on some of my police knowledge and life experience, I gladly jumped on the opportunity to assist. I ended up training ten new deputies during my two years as an FTO from 2007 to 2008.

Being a FTO was not an easy task. I was entrusted by my department to train brand new deputies and help mold them into someone who could perform every aspect of police work on their own. I started off the same way with all my trainees and that was by having a one-on-one meeting with them to go over what our department's expectations of them were and also what I expected from them during the coming months. I remind them that they would be in the field training program for the next four months depending on how well they do. If they met all the standards set forth by our FTO program, then it would be exactly four months before they got off FTO. If they struggle in certain area(s), and I felt like the issue(s) could be fixed, then I could recommend to my supervisor to extend them a few more weeks so I could try to correct the problem(s.) If it was something that could not be corrected, then the Sheriff could ask them to resign.

I knew being a new deputy and a trainee was going to be difficult in the beginning, because I had been a trainee myself when I first started. I knew the trainee was going to experience situations and circumstances that classroom scenarios at the academy could only touch upon. They probably saw and spoke about a certain scenario only a limited amount of time before moving on to the next scenario. Since every real life experience could go in any direction, scenarios in the academy were limited in their ability to prepare new deputies for the real situations. My job was not only to share my previous experience with the new deputies, but also to provide them with continuous training and supervision out in the field. I also assisted them with the acclimation into the law enforcement culture. One of the things that I did a lot as an FTO was I had to document their every action, whether it was right or wrong. I had to honestly rate and evaluate their abilities to perform as a deputy under real-life interaction with the public, criminals, the criminal justice system, and the trainee's performance in crisis situations.

I was not a high-stress FTO. I tend to mentor more than discipline. I like to explain to them what they did wrong and what they needed to do to correct the problem. I normally did everything hands-on since I believe that was a good way for most people to learn, but I would always evaluate each trainee to see which way would ultimately be the most effective to get my teaching across. I believe our FTO program was successful because the trainers we had were up to the task themselves. You can't become an FTO because you want the extra

5 percent in pay when you have a trainee. You become an FTO because you want to be one, to help mold the future of the department.

All of my trainees made it through their FTO programs and are now working solo and excelling at our department. I was just happy to be there to help them through their initial training. Hopefully, one day one of them could be the sheriff. After my FTO assignment was over and following the birth of my fourth daughter, Brynnleigh, I tested to be our next Family Violence Detective working in partnership with the Solano County Office of Family Violence Prevention Team (OFVP.) OFVP's coordinator was Carolyn. She had three people that worked in her staff: Stephanie, Sylvia, and social worker Susana. Within OFVP, they had the Family Violence Intervention Team (FVIT.) Susana was part of this team working with the detective from the Solano County Sheriff's Office. I was hoping to be that person from the sheriff's office to work with Susana.

In January 2009, I was selected to be a part of this great team. I would work with Susana as we mostly responded to help domestic violence victims after an incident to deal with the aftermath of a very stressful, sometime painful ordeal. I had no idea what I was getting myself into at the time. I quickly learned that this job was not for the weak-hearted. Sure, I have responded to hundreds of domestic dispute and assault calls during my nine years at South City, but as a first responder, you only see what is on the surface. Being a detective and dealing with interviewing the victims and suspects in depth afterward to try to find out what really happened has really opened my eyes. I had no idea about the dynamics behind domestic violence. How perpetrators use emotional abuse, isolation, intimidation, coercion, threats, male privilege, their children, economic abuse, and minimizing or blaming the victims for the incident. The things that Susana and I saw and the countless stories of continuous abuse that we heard from the victims were very heartbreaking. Domestic violence has a profound impact on families and communities as a whole. From our experience, domestic violence crosses all demographic and socioeconomic lines. It did not matter who you were. Anyone was prone to be a victim of domestic violence.

In my first six months working with Susana, we had already investigated over one hundred cases of domestic violence, child abuse, and elder abuse alone in Solano County. Investigating any child abuse case is always the hardest thing for us since we both have young children of our own at home. The kind of things we learned through our investigations that perpetrators would do to children is so heartbreaking and unfathomable, but they do happen. There were many times when we would ask each other how could someone do this to a child? Children are so innocent, and it's so disheartening to see so many of them lose that innocence at an early age due to physical or sexual abuse. I couldn't just come home and tell my wife all the sad things that I saw and learned at work. Sometimes I tried to talk to coworkers, but some of them don't really understand and would ask me why the victim didn't just walk away from the relationship. What some of them do not know is that victims usually do not have any places to go where they will be safe from their batterers. Because of the ongoing history of the abusive relationship, the batterer knows all of the victim's options and could follow. It takes money, a support network, and time for detailed planning to ensure that a victim can escape or "just walk away." That is exactly why sometimes victims feel they are safer staying with the batterer for the time being than trying to leave or escape. That is where Susana comes in. Susana is very good at what she does. She has been helping domestic violence victims get out of dangerous situations for a very long time. She is very knowledgeable when it comes to helping victims leave their abusive relationship. There are a wide variety of services Susana could offer a victim in order help the victim and their children escape their abusive relationships. For extreme abusive relationships, there are services where the victims could leave the area and start all over again elsewhere.

Susana and I were working really well together as a team. We were helping many victims and their children get away from their abusive relationships. Unfortunately, because of our hard economic times, the Solano County Board of Supervisors decided to cut funding for a lot of programs in July 2009, and my position was affected by these cuts. It was a very sad day for Susana and me as some of these victims will suffer, and there is no one there to really help them. I hope and pray that our economy will recover soon so we could get funding and restart this great service.

I am currently working as a general crimes detective. I work with a great group of folks. My overall boss is Lt. Elliott and my immediate supervisor is Sergeant Dewall. Both of these gentlemen possess a wealth of investigative knowledge and great leadership skills. They are definitely the deputies' leaders. I couldn't be any happier to be working for them. There are a total of four detectives currently assigned to the sheriff's investigation bureau. They are Detectives Curl, Elbert, McCants, and me. We are at half staff because of hard economic times. The partners I have now are definitely some of the top deputy sheriffs at our agency, so the people of Solano County would be in good hands should there ever be a big investigation. The conduit that keeps our investigation bureau clicking day in and day out is our Office Assistance III, Debbie. She does so much for our bureau, and she hardly gets the proper recognition she deserves. There are so many things she does for us that I could go on forever mentioning them.

As for my plans for the near future? Well, I do not know what The Supreme Architect of the Universe has in store for me, but I want to make Fairfield a permanent home for me and my family. Fairfield is a nice town to live out the rest of my life.

Brian (second from left) posing with his soldiers and the
Polish contingent during a live fire exercise 2003-2004

L to R – 1LT Stenn, Brian, 1LT Laughlin on a pass in downtown
Seattle, prior to deploying to Iraq, 2004

L to R – CPT Chan, LTC Wells, Brian, CPT Prasad at Ft. Lewis, WA, 2004

Brian at Camp Echo, Ad Diwaniyah, Iraq 2004-2005

Brian with an Iraqi policeman during a foot
Patrol in downtown Ad Diwaniyah, Iraq, 2004

Brian with Iraqi children in downtown Ad Diwaniyah,
Iraq, 2004-2005

Brian at a Tactical Humint Team Conference with Major Elliott
at Camp Echo, Iraq, 2004

Brian, 1SG Gunnerson, SGT Burgos and Specialist Crain
on foot patrol in Iraq, 2004

Officer Toscano and Brian posed for a picture prior to going in "Service."

Brian standing with his SWAT buddies at the South San
Francisco Police Department in 2006

Brian standing beside his patrol vehicle with
the Solano County Sheriff's Office, 2007

Bollibokka Camping, 2009, Denton, Denton's father, Ace, Dan,
Brian, Carlos, Greg and Jon, on their annual camping trip

Brian and friends enjoying a San Francisco
Giants baseball game, 2008

L to R – Fairfield Mayor Harry Price,
Former Fairfield School Board
President Abe Baustista, Brian,
and State Assemblywoman Mariko Yamada at Brian's and Jamie's
City Council fundraiser, 2009

L to R – Tom, Nikki, Brian and Patrick
enjoying a poker night

Brian and family enjoying their time in Las Vegas, 2009

Brian and his family in Fairfield, 2009

Why America?

WHILE IN IRAQ, SSG Salter and I would often have discussions about what it is that makes America the best country on Earth, and why people want to live here. There was an incident that made us realize why. The week that two Marine pilots went missing in Iraq (2005), U.S. intelligence in Iraq placed the second aviator in our Area of Operations (AO.) The first was gone, but there was hope that the second might still be alive. *We need to find him!* Working in an intelligence oversight office in Iraq Central South, we marveled at the computer responses to the message we sent to our tactical teams—everybody *frenziedly* wanted to find the downed flyer alive. Guarded hopefulness turned into reverential, guilty despair—the kind you feel attending the funeral of an unnoticed friend—when we discovered that God had other plans for that Marine. *Damn!* Another lost son, husband, or father. Had it been a woman, well, insert your gender-specific family role. It's the same. The loss was real, the pain unspeakable. Then the memories come, sweeter than a Rockwell rendering of maple syrup at breakfast on a winter's day.

Why, America? Why do this to your sons and daughters? Is it worth it? Is it worth giving our lives in a country whose allegiances shift like grains of ageless sand at the caprice of desert winds? Of this war, our public and our allies have doubts. Even the prosecutors of the war, in divisive arguments, disingenuous press releases, and leaked documents have doubts. Our nation is fractured between believers of artillery's staggering power (*meet force with greater force*) and believers of the equally eroding force of steady, unassailable reasoning. And believers of neither, we suppose one could argue any side, and be correct on *some* level. *Give war a chance!* Said somebody's T-shirt.

An Internet blog resonated a tune less dramatic, but no less whimsical: *No blood for . . . whatever it is Syria's got a lot of pros and cons will pepper you with figures to prove their grand legitimacy.* But it didn't answer, "Why, America?" So ask us, ground-pounders, flyboys, and blue jackets, men and women acquainted with the despair of war, the guilt of survival, and the pride of serving what we think.

But expect no crisp reply. In the question, we see speciousness. We refuse to have our answers massaged into factional messages. We will tell you—you would think the response odd—that we are not politicians, but soldiers, *Volunteers*. Most of us sense a purpose for being in Iraq. The daily grind commands our attention, but in the larger scheme, that is a minuscule matter. We follow orders and serve the nation's best interest as judged by the officials we voted into office.

We cannot question. We choose not to question. But we are not mindless automatons. When the time comes that we no longer believe in what we do, we walk. That is the majesty of our system, to which those Marines and nearly five thousand others so far gave the definitive testimonial. Do we want to go that way? No. We do not want our families facing that hellish grief. We want to come home, play with our kids, drink beer, attend college, build careers, make love, and make something of our lives. Do we know fear? Yes. Our bravado masks that fear.

We hide behind valiant unit slogans, clever axioms, even crude ditties, like "One weekend a month, my ass," to cope with danger and drudgery. We think not of passing into the next world, but simply of doing our job in the little corner of our AO. (But just in case, we took out extra insurance and wrote powers-of-attorney.) We wield instruments of death, hoping to give life a chance. Phony as that sounds to the flag-burner back home, we are giving him or her a chance. It's a bit simple-minded, our trade. But shielding the desecrator, extinguish his or her right to express disapproval of how government conducts business, *is* our job. We are soldiers—we really believe in that *stuff!*

Why, America? With our high crime rate, stricken educational systems, and (insert society ill.) The America I know is not flawless, yet its allure is unique and *multidimensional*. The quintessence of that allure is hard to capture. Forget purple mountain majesty. Ask why Bill Clinton and the elder Bush, political adversaries who shelved differences, flew halfway around the world to bring consequence to despairing victims of the Asian tsunami or the Haitian earthquake. Too high-ceilinged? Then ask Bravo Company's soldiers and other American military personnel driving Humvees at highway speeds, why they bother tossing candy at Iraqi kids lining the roadside, when there is little chance to savor expressions of gratitude. Why, America, with your indictments of avarice, imperiousness, impatience for things inconvenient, and unilateral action in the troupe of many? Argue these, argue Abu Ghraib, and again be right at some level. But being American means that the frailties of our passions, actions, or historical governance cannot reason away the vast and historic decency of our people, our ethos, and our soul.

We pursue self-preservation, but aim to advance others who do us no harm, though their good fortune might little benefit us. You think it matters to the okra grower in Cairo, Georgia, if the *souk* merchant in Cairo, Egypt, breathes freer air. Yet no other state or reign, in history, has pursued human worth to the extent that we have. Perfect America, isn't? But seeing America, when at peace and when at war, and watching the actions of the many, in its highest institutional form at judicial and legislative levels, and in its primordial core in the mire of foreign earth, I can tell you that America is still the best place to be from, or just to *be*. I have an answer, the thoughts of a humble soldier. Its plain incongruence might unhinge you. But—if only to honor our fallen, our injured, our predecessors, and our colleagues who regularly miss the opportunity to perform glorious acts, but wage the maddeningly dreary, day in, day out, in Iraq and Afghanistan, on the high seas and the gray skies, and anywhere else we fly our flag—listen for a moment. Because when you ask, "Why, America?" I simply must tell you: *Why not?*

Biography of Brian Wynn Huynh Travis

B RIAN WYNN HUYNH Travis was born as Hung Van Huynh in Phan Thiet, South Vietnam, on May 19, 1970. In March 1979, Brian, his elder sister, and brother boarded a small fishing vessel along with twenty-seven other refugees and fled Vietnam under the cover of darkness. After spending thirty days on the high seas with very little food and water, they were very fortunate to have landed on an island in Indonesia. Six months later, Brian, along with his siblings, was sponsored to the United States by his aunt and uncle.

They arrived at Travis Air Force Base in November 1979, and began a new life in the State of California. He and his siblings were placed with their aunt and uncle in San Mateo County, and that was where they spent the rest of their childhood. Brian is ever so grateful to our country for giving people like himself an opportunity for a new, healthy, and prosperous life.

Brian attended Hillsdale High School in San Mateo and later the Community College of San Mateo. Then in 2002, Brian obtained a Bachelor of Arts in Criminal Justice Management from Union Institute and University, Sacramento. In 2000, Brian and his wife Joy moved their family to Fairfield, where they have lived since.

Brian continues to be actively involved with the City of Fairfield Community. He is currently on the City of Fairfield Citizen Advisory Committee to the Tri-City Planning and Cooperative Group. He also serves on the Pedestrian Advisory Committee to the Solano Transportation Authority (STA). In 2008, Brian and other law enforcement members successfully organized the first ever Solano County Law Enforcement for Kids softball tournament to raise money for the Boys and Girls Clubs and other after-school programs. This event was a huge success.

Brian has been a dedicated public servant for most of his life. He enlisted with the California Army National Guard in 1993, because of a strong sense of American pride and a need to give back to the country that has given him and his family so much. He started as a Private and rose through the ranks during the past seventeen years of service. Brian is currently a captain in the U.S. Army Reserves and is assigned to the WARISC at Camp Parks, Dublin, California. He is a veteran of the Bosnia Conflict and is also an Iraq War veteran serving in Operation Iraqi Freedom. Brian is a decorated soldier from his time in service. One of the most prestigious awards he received was the Bronze Star for his exemplary service in Iraq from 2004 to 2005.

Brian is also a public servant in his civilian career. He became a police officer for the South San Francisco Police Department in March 1999. He served in various capacities from patrol, to SWAT operator, to working in their Downtown Bicycle Patrol Program. In 2006, Brian made the transition to Solano County Sheriff's Office and became a deputy. In 2008, Brian Travis was awarded "Solano County Deputy of the Year," which later helped him to be recognized as an outstanding deputy and selected to be a Sheriff's detective in 2009. Brian is currently a detective for the sheriff's office.

In 2009, Brian ran for the Fairfield City Council, because he deeply cared about the city and the people that live there. He wanted to take a more active role in helping his city be a strong a vibrant city again. Brian received thousands of votes, but unfortunately he did not win. However, Brian is now rich with knowledge and most likely will run for city council again in 2011. Brian has been married for thirteen years to wife Joy and has four beautiful daughters. They also have two awesome dogs.

References

(1) http://en.wikipedia.org/wiki/Vietnam_War
(2) http://en.wikipedia.org/wiki/Vietnam_War
(3) http://en.wikipedia.org/wiki/Paris_Peace_Accords
(4) http://www.ichiban1.org/html/history/1975_present_postwar/nvn_invasion_1975.htm

Made in the USA
San Bernardino, CA
02 November 2017